WINNING LONG-TERM GAMES

REPRODUCIBLE SUCCESS STRATEGIES TO
ACHIEVE YOUR LIFE GOALS

LUCA DELLANNA

Luca Dellanna

@DellAnnaLuca
Luca-Dellanna.com

First edition
April 2024 update
Luca Dell'Anna © 2024 – All rights reserved.

You only get one life.
Why spend it pursuing paths that might not work out?

ADVANCE PRAISE

"Gem upon gem of insight [...] a must-read [...] for all those who plan on being successful and who take the goal of achieving that success with the deadly, focused, and unwavering seriousness it deserves."

— *GUY SPIER, AQUAMARINE FUND MANAGER*

"A great book [...]

I recommend picking up a copy."

— *JIM O'SHAUGHNESSY, O'SHAUGHNESSY VENTURES CEO*

"Another masterpiece [...]

It exceeded my already high expectations [...]

It's that good."

— *SCOTT MITCHELL, OCEG CEO*

"I learned very much from it!

Luca's books have my highest highlight density."

— *LANCE JOHNSON, WHITEBOARD GEEKS CEO*

CONTENTS

Foreword   viii

PART I
WINNING LONG-TERM GAMES

1. The First Principle   3
2. The Second Principle   6
3. Plateauing   13
4. The terror of falling behind   15
5. What makes a good strategy?   20
6. The 3 properties of good long-term strategies   22
7. Designing a good long-term strategy   27
8. Optimizing your life   29
9. The path forward   31

PART II
ARE LONG-TERM STRATEGIES REALLY BETTER?

10. Better options   35
11. Survivorship bias   41
12. The Maximum Reproducible Return   45
13. The Distribution of Outcomes   47
14. Time horizon bias   49
15. The path forward   53

PART III
LEVERAGING THE LONG TERM

16. Long-term evaluations   57
17. Playing iterated games   63
18. Long-term iterated games   65
19. Long-term assets   67
20. The Goose and The Eggs   69
21. High- and low-quality success   72
22. The path forward   74

PART IV
DERISK, DERISK, DERISK

23. Learning from failure	77
24. Learn from the failures of others	79
25. Learn from your failures	81
26. Learn from future failures	83
27. Do not address every risk, but do consider every risk	88
28. When to stick with a project and when to abandon it	90
29. Inevitability	92
30. Increase Your luck	94
31. The path forward	96

PART V
HOLISTIC SUCCESS

32. Races to the bottom	99
33. Spillovers	104
34. Comparisons and the Pareto Frontier	105
35. Choose reproducible objectives	110
36. The 1% Life	112
37. Happiness rules	115
38. It's closer than we think	116

Conclusions	119
About the Author	125
Also by Luca Dellanna	127
Ergodicity	128
Best Practices for Operational Excellence	129
The Control Heuristic	130
Managing Hybrid and Remote Teams	131
100 Truths	132
The World Through a Magnifying Glass	133

APPENDIX

39. Fishbone Diagrams	137
40. Managing bets	141
41. Mixed Feelings	148
42. Committing to the long term	152
43. Committing to the long term while retaining flexibility	154
44. Learning & adaptation	155

45. Don't be too smart 159
46. Common goals and how to make them more
    reproducible 162

   Acknowledgments 169

FOREWORD

This foreword is written by Guy Spier, a Zurich-based investor and friend. He is the author of "The Education of a Value Investor" and the manager of the Aquamarine Fund.

While this foreword focuses on investing, this book will help you achieve long-term success however you define it, be it financial, professional, personal, or spiritual. In fact, the four are deeply interconnected. For example, as Guy himself noted, it is hard to make good investing and professional decisions if your life and relationships outside of work are unstable.

Precisely because of his acknowledgment of how the naive optimization of any single area of our lives is counterproductive, and of his awareness of how survivorship bias makes us underestimate the importance of playing the long game, Guy seemed the natural choice for the foreword of this book. So, I felt honored when he wrote one.

Enjoy the foreword and, then, the book.

Foreword

Berkshire Hathaway might be the most successful company that ever existed. What made it so successful? Many talk about the Berkshire Hathaway system - but what exactly is that? Simply to call it "Value Investing" is nowhere near enough. Most would prefer to fall back on Charlie Munger's ideas: worldly wisdom, avoiding human misjudgments and applying the ancient stoics in daily life. Ultimately, that Seneca, Marcus Aurelius and Epictetus are the source of Berkshire's success.

That is all true - but it misses key elements. One is that Warren and Charlie have always played long games. It's a truism. But what does it mean in practice?

Despite my having been a student of Berkshire Hathaway, Warren Buffett and Charlie Munger as long as most, and despite knowing that a key to success is to play long-term games, I did not understand the ideas behind this in granular detail.

Thankfully, help has come - from an unexpected source. Luca Dellanna is an Italian, from Turin, and is married to a Singaporean – in other words, far away from Berkshire Hathaway in Omaha.

Nevertheless, his new book, Winning Long-Term Games, has revealed to me many of the pieces of the puzzle that up to now remained obscured. Any student of value investing, of Buffett, Munger and Berkshire Hathaway, will uncover in Dellanna's book gem upon gem of insight into how Warren did it at Berkshire and furthermore will develop many insights and strategies for how to play long-term games in their own lives.

In short: it's a must read for all students of value investing, for all those who follow Warren and Charlie, and - most importantly - for all those who plan on being successful, and who take the goal of achieving that success with the deadly, focused and unwavering seriousness it deserves.

Guy Spier

PART I
WINNING LONG-TERM GAMES

"Both short- and long-term players have long-term goals and play short-term games.

The difference is that short-term players play short-term games to win them, whereas long-term players play short-term games to advance their long-term goals."

1

THE FIRST PRINCIPLE

The key to winning long-term games is to stop playing them as a succession of *separate* short-term games.

Yet, most people take the opposite approach.

Here are three examples:

1. The manager who sees each interaction with her team as a *separate* game. Every time she talks to her subordinates, it's to get things done rather than develop their skills. As a result, she fails to build the long-term assets (a competent team) she needs in order to win her long-term game (a successful career).

2. The spouse who lies as a way to avoid responsibility. If lying has, say, a 1% chance of getting discovered, it is a great short-term tactic (it succeeds 99% of the time) but a terrible long-term strategy (if you lie once a week, you have a 99.5% chance of getting caught over a decade).

3. The solopreneur who sends weekly emails to their mailing list and sees each as a *separate* game. They *consume* their audience's trust to generate more sales within a single email instead of *building* trust to create more sales within a few months.

These three examples show that **approaching long-term games as a succession of *separate* short-term games is a bad strategy** *despite working great over short time horizons.*

THE BETTER STRATEGY

…is to embrace the repeated nature of long-term games.

This doesn't mean proceeding slowly or delaying gratification; not at all. Instead, it means to **play short-term games not to win them but to increase your chances of winning the long-term game.**

For example,

- **Use short-term games to build long-term assets,** such as trust, know-how, habits, relationships, etc. Any success achieved without them won't last long.
- **Play iterated games.** Interact with people not to get the most out of each interaction but to improve the next interaction.
- **Take risks, but never risks that might ruin your long-term assets** (capital, trust, health, etc.).
- **Take on projects that might not work, but do it in such a way that even failure brings you closer to success,** e.g., building skills, self-knowledge, relationships, etc.

Notice the common thread. **Winning long-term games is not about going slow or avoiding short-term games.**

It is about playing short-term games *as parts* of long-term ones, not to win the former but to win the latter.

CHAPTER SUMMARY

This chapter illustrated the first principle to winning long-term games: **play short-term games not to win them but to progress your long-term objective.**

When considering how to play a given short-term game, examine the impact of all options on your longer-term goals and choose the one with the most positive influence.

Of course, sometimes, you need to win short-term games to progress your long-term goals, as when an important deadline is looming. But even then, how you choose to win the short-term game will significantly impact your long-term goals, and you should consider that.

Otherwise, you will find yourself winning short-term games but making no progress towards your long-term goals – a very frustrating situation.

———

This was the first principle to win long-term games.

The next chapter is about the second and last principle.

2

THE SECOND PRINCIPLE

You *can* win long-term games without addressing common causes of failure, but the chances are that you won't.

Over short time frames, it is different: you can get away by ignoring common causes of failure, and you probably will. For example, if you have a single two-month project, you can safely ignore burnout. Work on it as hard as possible; you won't burn out. But a whole career? That's a different thing.

As another example, over short time frames, you can ignore root problems. If your career isn't taking off because you lack some fundamental skills, in the short term, you can overcompensate by working harder. But that's not sustainable over extended time frames.

As a third and final example, a common reason people get stuck in their career after some initial success is a lack of a solid professional network. I'm not saying that you cannot succeed without a network of professional relationships; it's just that it's less likely you will succeed. So, if professional achievement is important to you, you should do what it takes to maximize your chances of success.

Can you spot the common thread across all three examples?

In all of them, thinking about how you might fail is superfluous in the short term – in the sense that, in the short term, risks are unlikely to materialize, and thus, any risk management activity appears to be a waste of time.

However, it is not superfluous over the long term, over which even unlikely risks have a significant chance of materializing.

Similarly, thinking about how you might fail is superfluous in the sense that you *can* succeed without addressing common causes of failure. Sometimes, people get lucky.

But it's not superfluous if you're unsatisfied with merely a chance at succeeding and want instead a *good* chance of success.

To have a good chance of winning long-term games, you must be aware of common sources of failure and do something about them before it's too late.

One way to become aware of common sources of failure is a technique called *pre-mortems,* where you imagine yourself in a few years, in a scenario where you failed, and ask yourself, "What could have caused me to fail, and what can I do about it now?"

Another way to become aware of common sources of failure is to examine how others who had a similar goal to yours failed. The following few pages discuss this.

22 COMMON REASONS YOU MIGHT FAIL

Here is an overview of 22 common reasons you might not achieve your long-term goals. Other parts of this book explore most of the list items in greater detail, but it is useful to summarize them here.

1. **You keep doing what brought you success at the previous stage of your life, even if it's not what you need to get to the next stage.** To move to the next stage, do what those at the next stage do even though you're not there yet.

2. **You do *some* of what's necessary to succeed, but not *everything* that is necessary.** For example, if you are a researcher and make a fantastic discovery but aren't good at communicating it, you limit your chances of success, celebrity, funding, and impact.

3. **You don't play the long term.** Instead of building a reputation, a community, a body of work, a portfolio of investments, a strong team, or other long-term assets, you spend all your time pursuing short-term strategies that leave you with nothing but a quick profit.

4. **You don't play iterated games.** You enter each meeting (with partners, customers, etc.) as if it were a one-off transaction. This is good if it is indeed a one-off transaction, but most interactions are actually iterated games (or should be). Approach them as such.

5. **You take excessive risks.** *Some* level of risk-taking is good and often necessary even. However, in some fields, such as sports and investing, there is a concept called the Maximum Reproducible Return: an optimal growth rate you can only exceed by taking risks that increase potential outcomes *but reduce average ones.* (More on this in a later chapter.)

6. **You do not take enough risks.** As a result, you limit your growth rate below the minimum level required to achieve your goals.

7. **You quit too early.** Some projects are like seeds: they can only grow so fast and require watering them for long enough before they blossom. It's okay to quit sometimes, but it is problematic if you *always* quit before doing what it takes to give a reasonable chance for your seeds to blossom.

8. **You never quit.** It is possible but unlikely that your first project, plan, or partner is the one that will work out great. More probably, you will have to try a few before one succeeds. This should be baked into your strategy.

9. **You progress too slowly.** By the time you notice, it's too late. You need a system to know when you should go faster.

10. **You try to be too smart.** Of course, creativity and innovation will help you, and for some pursuits, they are necessary. However, while some innovation is good, reinventing the wheel comes with large risks and costs of opportunity. Be considerate when choosing where to innovate and where to instead re-use what worked for others.

11. **You work for a bad boss, a bad company, with a bad partner,** or someone who limits your potential.

12. **You rely too much on yourself** and do not seek the help or support of others, therefore limiting your potential.

13. **You kill your Goose.** To get the proverbial Golden Eggs, you need to grow a Goose first: a reputation, a network, a team, a body of work, etc. However, when we see others producing Golden Eggs faster than us, we are tempted to squeeze our Goose to keep up, killing it in the process.

14. **You risk your Goose.** A subtle variation of the previous point, you take bets with a large upside but also a risk of killing your Goose in case of failure, e.g., making a risky investment, risking your reputation, or burning out your collaborators. Even if the bet has a positive expected value, if you take enough of them, eventually, you will kill your Goose. Good long-term strategies never put the Goose at risk.

15. **You do not know what you want, nor do you have a strategy to discover it.** If it takes you too long to find out what you want, you might lack the time to achieve it, or you might make it unlikely to happen.

16. **You want to succeed in a specific way.** You refuse opportunities for happiness or success that look different from your expectations. There is nothing wrong with being specific, but you must acknowledge that the more specific you are, the more opportunities you will miss and the less likely that you will eventually become successful.

17. **You have a non-reproducible definition of success.** For example, aiming to become #1 in a field with a lot of competition is non-reproducible by definition because all it takes for you to fail is a single person more determined or luckier than you. You *can* succeed under these conditions, but you cannot guarantee success.

18. **You envy or imitate non-reproducible success.** You adopt strategies that worked for someone but might not work for anyone – and you adopt them not with a "let's try" attitude but blindly following them.

19. **You have incompatible objectives.** You can become (nearly) anything, but you cannot become everything. List all your goals (professional, personal, etc.) and check whether you can *reproducibly* achieve them all together. If not, you might have to reconsider some.

20. **You compartmentalize success.** You blindly try to maximize achievement in one area of your life without noticing its negative impact on other areas of your life until it's too late.

21. **Your objectives are misaligned with your talents and dispositions.** While you *might* win an uphill race, it will be much more difficult than winning a downhill one. Moreover, it will require so much time and energy that it will negatively impact the rest of your life. The alternative is to embrace your talents and predispositions.

22. **You have mixed feelings about achieving your objectives.** For example, you want to become wealthy but also have mixed feelings about wealthy people. This might become a major limiting factor.

Of course, there are more reasons why people fail. Here, I just gathered twenty-two of the most common and actionable ones.

In addition to these, take a few minutes to think if there are other common reasons for failure specific to your long-term goal(s).

For example, if your long-term goal is to become a successful lawyer, think carefully about why people who studied law eventually failed to achieve this objective.

Be careful about thinking, "This problem won't apply to me because I'm smarter than them." Smartness is often judged post-hoc, so you do not know yet how smart or wise you really are.

If you do not think about how others failed,
you might succeed in a way that won't matter:
either your success will be short-lived,
or eclipsed by some larger problem you neglected.

PRACTICAL APPLICATIONS

Every now and then, I go through this list and ask if any of those points apply to my current strategy. That allows me to make the appropriate adjustments before it's too late.

Then, to prevent any blind spots, I also ask myself, "What are possible reasons why, in ten years, despite my current strategy, I might have failed to achieve my objectives?"

This question often gives me great insights into possible points of failure, therefore increasing my chances of success.

3
PLATEAUING

Only some of those whose trajectory looked up and to the right a few years ago maintained that growing trajectory. Others plateaued *(i.e., their growth stalled)* or even fell back to where they started.

Those whose trajectory continues growing built their early success on strong foundations. Conversely, those whose trajectory plateaued built their early success thanks to excessive risk-taking or taking shortcuts instead of building what's required to sustain success over time.

SHORT-TERM VS LONG-TERM PLAYERS

Short-term players only care about their rate of growth.

Long-term players also care about their growth rate, obviously, but only the portion that is achieved on solid foundations and is likely to continue in the future.

Long-term players do not care about unsustainable success.

MOVING TO THE NEXT STAGE

There is another common reason why people plateau. To understand what it is, let's look at the corporate ladder.

If you are an employee who's already good at your current job, working harder on it won't increase your chances of promotion much. Instead, what will move the needle is acquiring and displaying the skills that demonstrate you can handle your *next* job.

This principle applies to many other contexts. What brought you success at the current stage of your life is unlikely to be sufficient to bring you to the next stage. **You get to the next stage by displaying the skills and habits that people who are already at that stage display.**[i]

Whenever you feel stuck, ask yourself whether you're working on what brought you success instead of what will bring you success.

A good long-term strategy avoids plateauing by evaluating what to work on based not on current needs but on future ones.

This does not mean you should make rigid plans spanning decades; these might be counterproductive if assumptions change. Instead, it means that you should decide what to work on next based not on where you currently are but on where you want to go.

---

i. Of course, there are plenty of people who got promoted to the next stage without having demonstrated the skills it requires. But the fact that it is possible to get promoted this way doesn't mean it's likely that you will get promoted this way. Remember the Second Principle, and do not forget about survivorship bias.

4

THE TERROR OF FALLING BEHIND

If playing the long term is such a good strategy, why don't more people use it?

To answer this question, let's take a look at investing. A counterintuitive rule is that **if you grab merely-average market returns for above-average periods of time, you will get well-above-average outcomes.**[i]

Yet, few investors adopt this simple long-term strategy.

That's because every day, the resolution of long-term investors is tested by the news of some investor beating the market with some risky short-term strategy.

Of course, that strategy is likely to be worse – **short-term success is more likely due to luck or short-term optimization than competence.**[ii]

Yet, the feeling of falling behind is strong.[iii]

And **it is precisely this feeling of falling behind that makes many of us switch from good long-term strategies to bad short-term ones.**

BUT SHOULDN'T WE IMITATE THE SUCCESSFUL?

You shouldn't imitate all successful people, only those who succeeded using good strategies – strategies that can reliably bring success to those using them.

I often use the example of casino croupiers. They are the only people at the gambling tables with a money-making strategy, yet every day, they see at least one player get richer than them.

However, they must remind themselves that abandoning their job to become gamblers would be an error: they would make much less money.

If you must choose whose strategy to imitate, copy the croupiers, not the lucky players.

GOOD STRATEGIES AND BAD STRATEGIES

At the casino, it's easy to spot who the croupier is. In real life, it's harder.

How do you identify those with a plan worth imitating, and how do you differentiate them from those who just got lucky?

The first step is to **stop using short-term growth rates to estimate how good a strategy is.**

While indeed, on average, good strategies grow faster than bad ones, it is also true that it's easy to grow faster due to factors that are unsustainable over the long term, such as luck, excessive risk-taking, or behaviors with short-term benefits and long-term costs.

In fact, while it's true that amongst those growing fast, we will find plenty of skilled people, it is also true that amongst those growing very fast, we will find plenty of skilled people *who are also making short-term choices.*

As a result, **if we act upon the desire to emulate those growing faster than us, we are more likely to imitate short-term optimization than competence.**

Don't get me wrong! There's plenty to learn amongst those growing faster than us! But **never imitate unquestioningly, and only replicate those behaviors that make sense** *over the long term.*

SKILL AND LUCK

Of all the successful people, only a few succeeded using reproducible strategies. Instead, most succeeded using non-reproducible strategies: strategies that, if you imitated, you would only have a small chance of good outcomes. You shouldn't imitate those. *(Unless as a series of short-term projects within a longer-term strategy; I will expand on this point later.)*

The tricky part is that **people succeeding with non-reproducible strategies are often extremely intelligent and hard-working, which misleads us into believing that intelligence and hard work are sufficient to imitate their success. But it's often not the case.** Luck or other difficult-to-reproduce conditions are frequently required, too.[iv]

Don't get me wrong. A key skill in life is to learn how to harness luck. However, **we should differentiate between** *bets* **that might not work and** *strategies* **that might not work.** Do imitate risk takers, but only risk-takers who took bets *in the context of a good strategy* that, thanks to a good setup and a wise allocation of bets, none of which can fail ruinously, guarantees eventually achieving good outcomes.

Only use strategies that lead to good outcomes with almost certainty. (It is possible! A later chapter titled "*Inevitability*" will teach you how.)

CASE STUDY

According to a Morningstar study that analyzed 112 funds trying to beat a simple "60/40" investing strategy, only nine had better risk-adjusted returns than the 60/40 strategy.[v]

The wise conclusion would be that looking for *good* returns is more likely to work than looking for *great* ones.

Yet, most funds try to beat the market nevertheless, with the same arrogance with which 93% of drivers think they are better than average at driving. [vi]

The point is not that beating the market is impossible. There are a few great investors who do so consistently.

The point is that **because we look at success through the lenses of hindsight and survivorship bias, we constantly overestimate its reproducibility.**

And because we overestimate the reproducibility of short-term strategies, we switch from strategies with great long-term returns to worse ones.

HINDSIGHT BIAS

The previous case study showed a common yet faulty reasoning: **"Everyone who succeeds is smart, everyone who fails is dumb, and I am smart; therefore, I have a good shot at succeeding."**

The problem is in the use of hindsight to determine who's smart. It might lead you to underestimate the percentage of intelligent people who fail and, therefore, overestimate your chances of success.

The same faulty reasoning applies to our evaluations of strategies. **Of course, everyone who succeeded had a great strategy – if we use hindsight to determine how great a strategy is. That might lead us to overestimate how likely we are to succeed with a great strategy.**

It's not that great strategies aren't powerful. They obviously are! But it's hard to know what a great strategy looks like without relying on hindsight.

So, while having a great strategy is very helpful, the problem is that **it is hard to know whether your strategy is great before you try it.**

Therefore, checking whether it worked for others is a good idea only if you can pinpoint exactly which parts of their strategy and actions were signal and which noise – an incredibly hard task.

That said, the next chapter will help you precisely with this, giving you a few criteria for evaluating how good a strategy is without relying on hindsight.

---

i. Part of it is because of investors who accumulate losses so high that they must quit, and part of it is because an investment gone bad slows compounding ("Losses absorb future gains," I wrote in my book *Ergodicity*).
ii. Incompetent people outnumber competent ones, increasing survivorship bias risk.
iii. Falling behind can also have material consequences, such as investors fleeing to another fund.
iv. A further consideration is that some strategies offer reproducible outcomes but are still hard to reproduce because of *opacity:* **people emulating the strategy imitate its irrelevant parts and/or miss some key point.**
v. Source: "Tactical Funds Miss Their Chance," Morningstar, February 2, 2012.
vi. Source: "Are we all less risky and more skillful than our fellow drivers," O. Svenson, 1981.

5

WHAT MAKES A GOOD STRATEGY?

Looking at society, we see plenty of people who achieved quick or easy success. So, that becomes our standard for what a good strategy is, and we consider suboptimal any strategy that takes longer or requires more effort.

However, for every individual who achieved quick or easy success, there are many more who used the same tactic and failed. [i]

At the aggregate level, we do not care about a strategy's chances of success. For example, we do not care about everyone who has tried to become a pop star but failed. We only care about those who succeed.

But **at the individual level, we do care about a strategy's chances of success**, very much so. In fact, because we only have one life, a strategy's chances of success are its most important property, and speed and efficiency should be subordinate to it.

TACTIC RISK VS STRATEGY RISK

Before continuing, let me highlight a common misunderstanding.

Good strategies want certainty of success, but that doesn't mean they do not take gambles that might not work. In fact, plenty of good strategies rely on taking enough gambles so that at least one works.

The key is that **good strategies do take gambles, but only in ways that make sense in the long term.** They never take gambles whose failure might endanger future chances of success.

For example, long-term players might work on projects that might fail, but only in such a way that even a failure wouldn't endanger their reputation (e.g., never overpromising and always communicating transparently).

Tactics might be risky, but their risk must not transfer to the strategy.

Tactics might fail, but strategies must eventually guarantee success.

So, we have seen that good strategies almost guarantee success. But how can we know what strategies have this property?

In the next chapter, let's see the three properties of good long-term strategies that help achieve almost inevitable success.

---

i. The main exception is people entering novel fields where the lack of competition allows for fast, easy, and reproducible success, but only for a limited time before the field gets too crowded.

6

THE 3 PROPERTIES OF GOOD LONG-TERM STRATEGIES

Good long-term strategies have three properties.

1) They are sustainable. They do not require risks or sacrifices that you cannot take for long without severe consequences or that would clash with your other long-term goals.

2) They are constructive. They play iterated games and build, instead of consuming, the long-term assets that bring long-term success (such as trust, know-how, relationships, capital, etc).

3) They move towards inevitability. They proactively surface and address problems; they learn and adapt. They do not merely provide a *chance* of success but do what's required to almost *guarantee* it.

As you can see, **long-term strategies not only have a long-term time horizon but also embrace it and leverage it to achieve better and more certain outcomes than what a short-term strategy can reliably achieve.**

Over the next three pages, let's see the three properties in greater detail.

GOOD LONG-TERM STRATEGIES ARE SUSTAINABLE

Working overtime is a great tactic to maximize this week's productivity. Not only will you get more done, but a week of evenings spent working is unlikely to cause burnout or a divorce.

But work overtime every other week for several years in a row, and burnouts and divorces become much more likely.

Similarly, sending a sales email to your mailing list is a great tactic to increase sales. But if all you send to your mailing list is sales emails, people won't read your emails anymore.

Some tactics are useful but shouldn't become strategies: they are suited to short time horizons but not long ones. At most, they should be used sparingly and wisely as *parts* of a longer-term strategy.

This means that:

– Long-term strategies can contain risky projects, but those projects should only be risky in the sense that they might not work and never in the sense that their failure might endanger the strategy.

– Long-term strategies can use tactics that consume long-term assets (such as health and trust) but must use these tactics sparingly and alternate them to enough periods of building the assets they consume.

GOOD LONG-TERM STRATEGIES ARE CONSTRUCTIVE

If you have three shots to throw a ball in a distant hole, it doesn't make sense to use all three shots to attempt a hole-in-one. Instead, use the first shot to get closer to the hole so that the other two shots are more likely to go in.

Similarly, too many people fail to achieve their life goals because they spend years working on projects that are "hole-in-one shots."

Not only do "hole-in-one" projects have low chances of success, but when they miss, they do not make the following projects more likely to succeed.

If you have a long-term horizon to achieve a goal, it doesn't make sense to use tactics that are optimal for holes-in-one. You want to use strategies optimal for a hole-in-three. Strategies that progressively get you closer to your goal.

Ask yourself: what assets (skills, habits, relationships, resources, etc.) would make your future projects more likely to succeed?

Long-term strategies take the time to build these long-term assets, *even when it doesn't seem like a good moment to do so.*

―――――

"The key to success is to spend more time on important-yet-not-urgent activities than most of your peers."

GOOD LONG-TERM STRATEGIES ARE INEVITABLE

Many long-term strategies are variations of the following: do a few projects that might fail, but do them in such a way that failure doesn't compromise future projects, and in such a way that even in failure, you still build know-how, trust, and relationships. If you do so, eventually, you will succeed.

As you can see, **good long-term strategies often include projects that might fail,** *but only in the context of a strategy that cannot fail.*

Do not take the "cannot fail" too literally. Whether a 100% success rate is possible is irrelevant. What matters is not to be satisfied with less than that and continuously ask yourself, "What might cause me to fail, and what can I do about it?"

Asking that question might reveal that you are taking too many risks or perhaps not enough.

It might reveal that you are going too fast, skipping steps, or perhaps that you are being too slow or complacent.

It might reveal that there is some lesson you don't want to learn.

It might reveal that there is some help you refuse to ask.

It might reveal that you're using the wrong strategy.

From that one question, you might learn a lot.

―――

The point is, never treat your strategy as you would treat a tactic. You can tolerate tactics that might not work, but you cannot tolerate strategies that might fail.

After all, you only get one life. **Make your strategy inevitable.**

BAD LONG-TERM STRATEGIES

We have seen the three properties of good long-term strategies: they are sustainable, constructive, and make success inevitable.

The next chapter will help you use these three properties to produce a good long-term strategy. For the moment, let's see a few red flags of having designed a *bad* long-term strategy:

- **It is not sustainable:** it might bring you some early growth but cannot sustain it over time.
- **It is not constructive:** it doesn't build the long-term assets required for long-term success.
- **It is not inevitable:** it might lead you to success but might also not.
- **It is not actionable:** it has no clear next step you can work on today.
- **It relies on the future not changing:** it doesn't incorporate learning and adaptation.
- **It focuses on a single area of your life and neglects the rest.** It might bring you to a *pyrrhic victory,* in which you achieve your objective, but it might still not matter because you compromised another important area of your life.

There are more red flags of a bad long-term strategy, but the above ones are the most important, and adding more to the list would dilute it and make it worse.

7

DESIGNING A GOOD LONG-TERM STRATEGY

Going through life without a strategy is like going through a forest without a compass. Sure, you *might* get out eventually, but probably not where you hoped to be.

That said, while I believe in long-term strategies, I do not believe in long-term *plans*. They tend to look good in theory but have blind spots and are fragile in an ever-changing environment.

For me, it's not much about designing a strategy top-down but rather iterating your current strategy by asking yourself the following questions over and over:

- Can I sustain my strategy long enough to guarantee success? If not, what changes should I make?
- Does my strategy build enough long-term assets to guarantee success? If not, what changes should I make?
- Does my strategy merely give me a chance to succeed, or does it guarantee it? If not, what else should I do?

AN ITERATIVE PROCESS

Of course, it is hard to answer these questions with precision and certainty.

But that's not the point. The point is that by asking yourself these questions once a week or once a month for long enough and answering them with honesty and humility, you dramatically increase your chances of success.

DO NOT REINVENT TOO MANY WHEELS

A common mistake at this stage is to "reinvent the wheel too much" or "try to figure it out yourself too much." Don't get me wrong, creativity and personal initiative are great! But you only have so many years to achieve your goals. So, **while some level of making mistakes and learning from them is good, you cannot afford to make too many mistakes or proceed too slowly.**

Find the right balance. **Reinvent one wheel but not all four. And use personal initiative, but only after having analyzed how others failed.**

Always look at your trajectory and ask yourself whether it's pointing towards where you want to be within an acceptable time frame – and if not, make the appropriate adjustments.

Note: I expanded the contents of this page in the Appendix chapter titled "Don't be too smart."

8

OPTIMIZING YOUR LIFE

At this point in the book, I should reiterate a key point from the first chapter, which began with, "The key to winning long-term games is to stop playing them as a succession of *separate* short-term games."

A similar principle from business operations – one of my fields of expertise – is as follows: "**If you optimize each component of the system individually, you won't have an optimal system.**"

Of course, the problem is not optimization itself but the type of optimization. **To have an optimal system, optimize the components *for their effect on the system,* not just their direct output.**

So, optimize your short-term goals and how you achieve them for how they progress your long-term objectives. This often means optimizing each short-term goal only up to a certain point. After all, there is such a thing as over-optimization, which happens when you optimize falsely assuming a static system or mistakenly neglecting externalities invisible in the short term but significant in the long term.

OPTIMIZE YOUR DISTRIBUTION OF OUTCOMES

There are a few possible ways to optimize for your long-term objective.

1. Maximize the best-case scenario – e.g., you aren't satisfied with becoming wealthy, but you also want to amass as much wealth as possible.
2. Achieve your objective as fast or as efficiently as possible – e.g., you are not satisfied with becoming wealthy, but you also want to do so with as little work as possible and as fast as possible.
3. Maximize your chances of achieving your goal – e.g., you aren't satisfied with having a chance at achieving your objectives, but you want to be as certain as possible that you will achieve and sustain them over time.

The three optimizations above are at odds with each other. You can pick one, but you cannot pick all three.

My suggestion, and my choice in life, is to optimize for the third option. I prefer making sure that given ten possible futures, I'm happy in all of them, rather than maybe being very happy in one, moderately happy in seven, and unhappy in two.

I optimize my distribution of outcomes.

That said, of course, you can make a different choice.

But do acknowledge it is a choice. And do choose wisely and deliberately.

9

THE PATH FORWARD

So far, we have seen the importance of not only having long-term objectives but, more importantly, the importance of achieving them through long-term strategies.

At this point, you might be convinced of the benefits of long-term strategies but still not be looking forward to implementing them instead of shorter-term strategies: after all, don't you want to succeed as fast as possible?

Hence, let's move to the next chapter, which answers the question of whether long-term strategies are really better than short-term ones.

PART II

ARE LONG-TERM STRATEGIES REALLY BETTER?

Some believe that playing long-term strategies is lazy or excessively conservative. Usually, that's because they look at driven people and notice that most of them use aggressive short-term strategies.

However, driven people who use long-term strategies consistently achieve better results than driven people who use short-term ones *at the net of survivorship bias*. Hence, playing long-term strategies is not lazy nor conservative but rational and ambitious. *(I will discuss survivorship bias later.)*

Moreover, people using long-term strategies also achieve their objectives in a more fulfilling way and without side effects that might damage other areas of their lives.

This chapter will demonstrate the hidden benefits of long-term strategies and prove that they are superior to short-term ones.

10

BETTER OPTIONS

Imagine one of your life objectives was to become a millionaire. And imagine you want to achieve it *by tomorrow*.

What could you do to succeed? Invest your life savings in lottery tickets? Attempt a heist? **A short time horizon constrains you to bad options.**

Now, imagine you gave yourself two years to become a millionaire.

What could you do? Take risky bets on the stock market? You would have better odds than in the previous scenario, but it would still be risky.

And what if you had thirty years to become a millionaire?

You would have plenty of relatively safe options, such as a good career and periodically investing your savings without having to take excessively risky bets.

The longer your time horizon, the better and more reliable your available options to achieve your goals. [i]

A BETTER LIFE

A common misconception about playing the long game is that it means delaying gratification. I strongly disagree.

If you give yourself more time to achieve your goals, you can make your journey towards success more pleasurable. Playing the long game, you will have less transactional relationships, will feel less pressure to take bad risks or trespass your boundaries, and will have the time to take very fulfilling long-term actions such as learning and honing your craft.

Note that this is not an invitation to slacking. Rather, it's the realization that hard work with a long time horizon is more pleasurable and fulfilling than hard work with a short time horizon.

Long-term strategies are constructive, sustainable, and inevitable – three qualities that lead you to take actions that ultimately improve satisfaction, such as learning, building trust, having fun, and resting every now and then.

Playing the long game has nothing to do with delaying gratification – only with delaying comparison. You must resist the temptation to compare yourself with others based on your short-term growth rate or temporary success.

Ideally, avoid all comparisons, but if you must, **compare yourself only against those who are also playing a long game.** Those who are also unwilling to trespass on their values, take excessive risks, or over-focus on a single area of their life to the detriment of others.

Never compare yourself to someone with a shorter time horizon. Doing so will mislead you into making suboptimal choices.

COMPOUNDING AND OUTLASTING

> "If your investment returns are in the 50th percentile every year, you will probably end up in the top 5-10% over a 20-year period."
>
> — *MORGAN HOUSEL*

Do not underestimate the power of compounding. Assets that produce over time more of the same asset (money, skill, audiences, etc.) grow faster the more you have. **Instead of competing for the fastest growth rate now, compete to have the fastest *reproducible* growth rate *over time.***

Similarly, do not underestimate the power of outlasting your competition. When you begin your career in a new field, you will be one of thousands with no previous experience. But as time passes by, you will become one of hundreds with some experience, and eventually one of a few with great experience.

While it won't necessarily get easier,[ii] the upside you get from staying in the game will grow.

The benefits of compounding and outlasting are so large and easy to reproduce that they are integral parts of Winning Long-Term Games.

These benefits of compounding are evident when it comes to money, but they also apply to relationships (e.g., the more people you know, the more events you will be invited to, and the more relationships you will get to make) and skills (the more you can do, the more you will try and, therefore, learn).

Conversely, the benefits of *outlasting* are less known but not any less important. Often, you might have ideas the world is not ready for (in the sense that there is not yet enough demand or infrastructure to support it); in this case, staying in the game will help you be there when the time is right, and you can finally profit.

Similarly, many investors became rich, not much thanks to their performance during bull markets, but thanks to their resilience during bear markets, which enabled them to be buyers at the bottom and thus acquire plenty of assets at great prices for their value.

There is plenty of value in outlasting your competition. However, this value is only visible if you adopt long-term evaluations.

"Ninety percent of success can be boiled down to consistently doing the obvious thing for an uncommonly long period of time without convincing yourself that you're smarter than you are."

— SHANE PARRISH

A SHORT-TERM FOCUS REDUCES YOUR POTENTIAL

Another common reason people do not embrace the long-term nature of long-term games is that they think, "If I play each short game trying to become successful as fast as possible, I might fail a few times, but earlier or later, I will succeed, and that will happen faster than if I played the long game."

I strongly disagree. **A pernicious property of playing short-term games as if they weren't part of a long-term game is that they do not make you progress in case of failure – and sometimes even in case of success!**

There are plenty of people who accumulate small successes after small successes yet fail to make any significant advancement. Think about the person who has lots of success dating but fails to convert any of that into a long-term relationship, or the entrepreneur who closes many sales but fails to get any repeated customers. Their short-term focus causes them to win in a way that doesn't create progress.

Conversely, there are long-term players who accumulate failure over failure *and nevertheless progress*. Their long-term focus ensures that even in failure, they build skills, understanding, and relationships that help them succeed eventually.

And there are people who accumulate short-term successes obtained through long-term focus, and these grow the fastest.

Playing without a long-term focus reduces your potential.

THE PROBLEM WITH CHASING FAST SUCCESS

Short-term players almost see winning long-term games as a failure. "You could have achieved that faster."

So, short-term players take actions that are unsustainable over the long term. They sacrifice their health or personal lives, incur excessive spending, consume their trust capital, take small risks that could go wrong in serious ways, and so on.

Conversely, long-term players only use strategies that they can sustain over the long term.

Like everyone else, long-term players try to win as soon as possible, but unlike everyone else, they do so without using strategies that compromise the long term.

They know that while it's *possible* to win in the short term, only long-term strategies can (almost) guarantee success.

---

i. Many social rituals, such as marriages and long-term employment, are about lengthening the time horizon to open better options and encourage long-term evaluations.

ii. You will have fewer competitors, but they will be fiercer. Early on, you competed mostly against mediocre players; as the game goes on, the mediocre drop, and you compete more and more against stronger players. This concept will be elaborated in the chapter titled *"Races to the Bottom."*

11

SURVIVORSHIP BIAS

Some strategies appear better than they are because of a phenomenon called survivorship bias – in which we overestimate how good a strategy is because we only look at those who used it and became successful but not at those who used it and failed.

Survivorship bias is particularly treacherous because of a phenomenon I call *hindsight gerrymandering,* which works as follows.

Imagine you go to the casino with ten friends, and you all play a few rounds of roulette, albeit each with a different strategy: one of you only bets on red, another one keeps betting on the 36, a third one always bets on the last winning number, and so on. After twenty minutes, you notice that all of you have lost money, except for one friend who always bet on the last winning number – he doubled his money.

What is your conclusion? Is it that playing Roulette is likely to lose you money? Or is it that betting on the last winning number is a great strategy for playing Roulette?

If you concluded the latter, you would be wrong. You committed *hindsight gerrymandering*: you used hindsight to draw boundaries between strategies that are actually all instances of the same bad strategy: participating in a money-losing game.

In the previous example, the use of hindsight is obvious. That's because everyone knows that Roulette is a game of pure luck and because the odds are known and in favor of the casino.

But when it came to other "games" where winners are due to a mix of skill and luck, such as the stock market, it is much easier to commit hindsight gerrymandering without noticing and thus fall prey to survivorship bias.

For example, imagine that one year, one investor becomes particularly successful. Other investors review his trades and notice that all his most successful investments were in companies with foreign CEOs. Suddenly, there might be a tendency to believe that investing in foreign CEOs is a great strategy! But, unless this strategy was known *before the fact,* it might be the result of randomness. Maybe that successful investor didn't even notice he was investing in companies with foreign CEOs or didn't think it was that important! And if other investors use hindsight to define strategies, they set themselves up for disappointment when, next year, the good performance of that strategy doesn't replicate.

In fact, **using hindsight to draw an inexistent boundary between a good and a bad strategy is the most common reason that otherwise very smart investors temporarily forget survivorship bias and get lured into adopting money-losing strategies.**

But there's another mechanism that makes survivorship bias hard to detect, and I will cover it on the next page.

A NUMERICAL EXAMPLE

Imagine two entrepreneurs, Alice and Bob. They each open a business with an initial capital of $100,000. Alice takes more risks and, as a result, has a high growth rate of 10%. However, because of those risks, she also has a high failure rate of 5%. Conversely, Bob takes less risks. As a result, his growth rate is lower, 8%, but so is his failure rate, 1%.

Who do we expect to make the most money: Alice or Bob?

The answer is counterintuitive: **Alice is more likely to be wealthier than Bob, yet we expect Bob to end up wealthier.**

Let me explain.

If we consider periods of a single year, Alice is expected to be wealthier than Bob 95% of the time. Yet, if you compare the expected wealth, Alice's is 95% times $100,000 times 110% = $104,500, whereas Bob's is 99% times $100,000 times 108% = $106,920. Bob's expected wealth is higher than Alice's despite him being less likely to be wealthier than her.

Here is another way to see it. Given a hundred Alices and a hundred Bobs, the top 95 wealthiest entrepreneurs would all be Alices. Yet, on aggregate, Bobs would have more wealth.

Survivorship bias makes us think that Alice's strategy is better because all the winners are Alices, but her strategy is not better. **Alice's strategy has higher potential but is less reproducible; therefore, she ends up worse, at the net of survivorship bias.**

RUNNING A SIMULATION

I ran a Monte Carlo simulation,[i] computing the results of ten million Alices and ten million Bobs running their businesses *for ten years* (using the same parameters as the previous example).

The results of the simulation are telling.

The top 10% of entrepreneurs by wealth are all Alices! That gives the impression that Alice's strategy is worth imitating more than Bob's.

And yet, the average Alice has only $155,000, whereas the average Bob has $195,000. Bob ends up 26% wealthier despite not appearing in the top decile even once!

What's even more surprising is that, if we only consider the surviving Alices (i.e., those who didn't fail), their average wealth is a whopping $259,000, whereas the wealth of the average surviving Bob is only $195,000. However, we shouldn't look at only the surviving Alices – we should look at *all* of them.

This experiment shows how misleading survivorship bias is.

The strategy producing the most winners is not always the best strategy for you.

---

i. The code for this simulation and the others in this section of the book can be found at https://github.com/lucadellanna/Alice-and-Bob.

12

THE MAXIMUM REPRODUCIBLE RETURN

As an investor, achieving the average market returns is a pretty good strategy: it's relatively cheap, doesn't take much effort, and produces better returns than apparent. After all, we have already seen that **if you achieve average returns for an above-average amount of time, you receive well-above-average returns.**

With some skill and hard work, you can even achieve returns that are slightly above the market. However, there is a limit to the returns you can achieve without taking excessive risks.

If you were alone, you would stop once you achieve the Maximum Reproducible Returns – the highest growth rate you can get without excessively risking irreversible losses.

However, you are not alone. Every day, there are investors earning more than you. You feel left behind.

They're using non-reproducible strategies, but you don't see that. They're earning higher returns by taking higher risks than you, but you don't see that. Or you see that, but the success of some of them makes you feel that those risks aren't that high.

Either way, you have a choice. Either you stick to your strategy and keep reaping the Maximum Reproducible Returns. Or you copy their strategy and, for a while, enjoy higher returns, until one day, inevitably, the risks you ignored materialize and generate losses big enough to offset all the extra profits and then some more.

Much of being a great investor consists of putting in the hard work and effort required to achieve the Maximum Reproducible Return *and then ignoring anyone who earns more than that, knowing that, eventually, they will crash.*

Note that the above is not fully true. First of all, you never want to fully ignore your competitors. You always want to check whether they're doing something right that's worth learning from.

Also, note that not everyone who uses a Non-Reproducible Strategy crashes. Some succeed. Some even triumph. But only *some*.

If the Maximum Reproducible Returns are, say, 10%, of course, there will be someone who reaps 12%. Of course, you *could* reap 12%. This doesn't mean that if you pursued those returns, you *would* earn them.

What matters is not the Maximum Possible Outcome but the Distribution of Outcomes.

13

THE DISTRIBUTION OF OUTCOMES

When you see someone achieving extreme success, or achieving success extremely fast, you only see one of many parallel worlds.

The question is, given ten parallel worlds in which that person uses the same strategy, in how many of them would they achieve success?

If the answer is ten, congratulations! They were probably using a Reproducible Success Strategy, and you might want to learn from them.

If the answer is less than ten, then they were using a non-Reproducible Success Strategy. Imitate them at your peril.

Do not judge strategies based on their best-case scenario[i] **(which, because of survivorship bias, is probably what you observe). Instead, judge strategies based on their distribution of outcomes.**

Good strategies only have satisfactory long-term outcomes – both in case of good and bad luck. *(How they can achieve this will be covered later, but here is a hint: they are designed so that they never put your long-term assets at risk, and so that even failures grow them.)*

AN EXAMPLE OF THE IMPORTANCE OF THE DISTRIBUTION OF OUTCOMES

Let's use the lottery as an example of why estimating the distribution of outcomes of a strategy is more important than estimating its expected value. *(As a reminder, the expected value of a strategy is the average of its outcomes.)*

The reason most of us do not play the lottery is because the expected value of purchasing a ticket is negative. For example, if a ticket costs $1 and you have a one-in-a-billion chance of winning a hundred million, the expected value of buying the ticket is -$0.90.

But what if the expected value of playing the lottery were positive? For example, what if you had a one-in-a-billion chance of winning 10 billion?

The expected value of buying a ticket would be +9$. Yet, you should still not play the lottery.

The reason is that if you spent $1,000 to buy a thousand tickets, you would still only have a one-in-a-million chance of winning 10 billion and a 99.9999% chance of losing $1,000.

And if you spent a million? You would have a 0.1% chance of becoming a billionaire and a 99.9% chance of losing a million. Not a good bet, unless you are already so wealthy as to not care about losing a million.

What matters is not the expected value of a bet but its distribution of outcomes.

---

i. The best-case scenario is an important factor in evaluating *tactics* but is much less important when evaluating *strategies*.
   Again, you want to take high-upside bets! But only if their downside doesn't prevent you from taking many of them, so that even if each bet is individually unlikely to succeed, a strategy of bets is likely to succeed.

14

TIME HORIZON BIAS

In the previous chapters, I introduced a concept of paramount importance: a strategy optimal for short time horizons might fail to produce good returns over long ones, and a strategy optimal for long time horizons seems inefficient over short ones.

Without a strong belief in this concept, you might be tempted into imitating short-term strategies that come with a high but unsustainable growth rate. Doing that might set you back over the long run.

So, let's see a numerical example that will demonstrate this counterintuitive principle. Imagine two *solopreneurs*, Alice and Bob, who try to grow their social media audience by writing engaging posts.

They both start with zero followers. Alice is more aggressive and uses lies and exaggerations to grow faster. As a result, she gets an average of 100 followers per post, but has a 5% chance that her lie is discovered, leading to a 20% loss of followers. Conversely, Bob never lies, but only grows at a rate of 50 followers per post – half of Alice's.

They both post once a day. Who do we expect to have the most followers? Think about the answer, then read the answer on the next page.

The right answer is that it depends on the time frame considered.

As you can see in the chart below, Alice's strategy has the advantage during the first month or so, whereas after that, Bob is expected to have more followers.

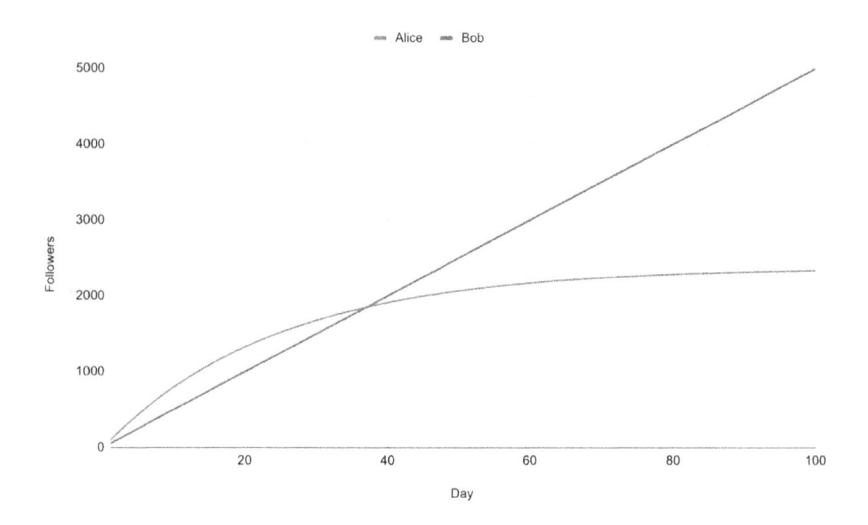

Of course, this is just a thought experiment. In real life, we would expect things to work differently: for example, Alice might learn from her mistakes, followers do not grow linearly, and so on.

Yet, the core point remains – a strategy performing better over short time frames might be suboptimal for long time frames.

Hence, **do not extrapolate long-term performance from short-term one, but always ask yourself how the short-term performance is achieved:** performance obtained through excessive risk-taking is unlikely to sustain over time.

TIME HORIZON BIAS AND SURVIVORSHIP BIAS

Let me link this chapter to the one on survivorship bias by noting that, in this thought experiment where Alice and Bob grow their social media following, Alice has only a 10% chance of getting more followers than Bob after 100 days. That would still mean that, given 100 Alices and 100 Bobs, the top 10 influencers by social media followers are all Alices! Even though Bobs are expected to have more followers on average. Again, beware of survivorship bias.

That said, because the rewards of social media disproportionally accrue to the top influencers, some readers might still be thinking: "I'd rather get a 10% chance of becoming a top influencer than a 100% chance of having a good-but-not-great following."

Yes, but also consider that 10% is the chance of being a top influencer after 100 days, whereas after 200 days, those chances go below 1%, and after a year, below 0.01%. [i] You don't want a mere 0.01% chance.

Of course, this is an exaggerated thought experiment. But the point remains: **when we observe someone becoming successful fast, we observe a suboptimal level of risk-taking than what would be optimal for a longer time horizon and at the net of survivorship bias.**

Those are levels of risk-taking that are optimal for "taking many people and selecting the best." But you cannot do that with yourself: your n is 1. Hence, adjust optimal risk-taking accordingly.

PRACTICAL APPLICATIONS

Always evaluate how good a strategy is over the relevant time horizon, never over a shorter one.

If you are an investor, do not compare the yearly returns of two strategies; instead, compare the expected long-term outcomes of using them for the next decade or so (or even longer).

If you are an entrepreneur, notice that there are activities, such as training, maintenance, and building a solid organizational culture, that look like waste in the short term but are absolutely necessary for a high chance of long-term success.[ii]

If you are a salesperson, the best tactic to close a sale today might not be the best tactic to getting a lifetime customer: the former benefits from destroying trust, and the latter from building it.

If you are an employee, spending the least effort to do your job is the best tactic to get through the day, but it also sets you up for a career made of mediocre days. Instead, consider allocating some effort to learning, improving, building relationships and trust, and so on.

Winning long-term games requires managing long-term risks, *even if they seem small in the short term,* **and building long-term assets,** *even if they seem unprofitable in the short term.*

CHAPTER SUMMARY

Strategies that work well in the short term might fail to work over the long term. And strategies that are optimal for the long term might seem inefficient over the short term.

To win long-term games, compare strategies over their long-term effectiveness and neglect their short-term one.

This doesn't mean never doing things that make sense in the short term. It means doing things that make sense in the short term in a way that doesn't endanger the long one. And it means doing things that don't make sense in the short term but are required to succeed in the long term, such as managing long-term risks and building long-term assets, even when it doesn't seem the best moment to do so.

---

i. Source: https://github.com/lucadellanna/Alice-and-Bob.
ii. In evaluating the truth of this statement, remember survivorship bias.

15

THE PATH FORWARD

In the first part of this book, we have seen how the key to winning long-term games is to embrace their long-term nature.

Stop playing them as a succession of separate short-term games.

Start playing them as a succession of *intertwined* short-term games, each of which is played not for its immediate outcome but for how it helps progress your long-term objectives.

The next part of this book will help you apply these principles to your life.

A FEW NOTES, BEFORE WE MOVE TO PART 3

First of all, if you have any questions, you can always write to me at **Luca@Luca-Dellanna.com** – I read all emails personally and usually reply within 48 hours.

Secondly, feel free to share attributed screenshots of this book on your social media. The more these ideas spread, the better!

Lastly, if you are interested in purchasing bulk copies of this book (e.g., for your friends, colleagues, or students), please email me.

PART III
LEVERAGING THE LONG TERM

Good long-term strategies do not merely have a long time horizon but also leverage it to take actions that are unavailable to shorter-term players.

For example, both a short- and a long-term player might aim to retire wealthy. The difference is that the short-term player aims to make quick bucks and, therefore, will not take actions without good short-term returns. Conversely, the long-term player is willing to forego short-term gains if doing so allows for better long-term gains.

But what exactly are such long-term actions, and how can you take them effectively?

This is the object of the third part of this book: how to take long-term actions.

16

LONG-TERM EVALUATIONS

Both short-term and long-term players have long-term objectives. Because of that, they both believe they are long-term players.

However, **what makes a long-term player is not the time horizon of their objectives but that of their evaluations.** Only long-term players consider the long-term impact of their actions (or lack thereof). [i]

The previous chapters illustrated some ways in which long-term games require different evaluations than what is effective for short-term ones. The problem with short-term evaluations is not that they are wrong (they are not). It's that **short-term evaluations get you stuck into winning short-term games without making any progress toward your long-term objectives.**

This chapter explains how you can make longer-term evaluations.

LONG-TERM ASSETS

If you are a manager or entrepreneur, you always have something urgent to do: a deadline to meet, a target to achieve… it never feels like a good moment to train your team.

Yet, your potential is capped by the talent of your team. If you never train them, they will never perform at the level required to support your ambitions.

Training never makes sense in the short term (there is always something more urgent to do) yet it is indispensable for long-term success.

This is a common paradox. **Building long-term assets** (such as skills, habits, relationships, etc.) **never makes sense in the short term** (there is always a faster way to meet short-term objectives), **yet it is necessary for long-term success.**

Your success is capped by your long-term assets. Increase your long-term assets, and you automatically increase your long-term potential.

However, **building long-term assets requires making long-term evaluations in the face of short-term pressures** – that's the price of long-term success.

PRACTICAL APPLICATIONS

You *might* have a tiny chance of achieving success without building long-term assets. But you cannot count on it. So, you should work on building the long-term assets required by your ambitions.

First of all, make a list of the long-term assets that help you achieve your long-term objectives. Think about skills, habits, relationships, trust, a track record, a portfolio, a healthy body, etc.

Then, acknowledge that you will have to start building those assets *now* – even if it doesn't feel like the right time, because it will never feel like the right time.

Of course, it doesn't mean you should stop your life to only work on the long term – that is often impractical or counterproductive. Instead, it means **you should dedicate at least a couple of hours a week to doing things that do not make sense in the short term but are required for the long term.**

A good practice I recommend to my consulting clients is to block some time in their schedule to work on the long term every week or every month. For example, I know of a few companies who reserve, e.g., the second Friday of the month, to only work on long-term problems, such as building competencies, automating procedures, discussing long-term risks, and so on.

Start doing what doesn't make sense now but is required for the long term – your Future Self will thank you.

OVER-OPTIMIZATION

If you ever find yourself in a ski race, it's relatively easy to be the fastest skier down a single slope: just crouch yourself in a bullet position, keep your skis as parallel as possible, and keep doing it as long as you can – even as everyone else prepares for the next turn. You will eventually crash, because you over-optimized for the straight part of the slope and won't be able to survive the turn. But until then, you will be the fastest one. *(Obviously, do not follow this advice.)*

It's a stupid strategy. Yet, plenty of people adopt it in business and life.[ii] They use over-optimization as a shortcut to success, even if it means being unprepared for what comes next. Even worse – their early successes cause them to focus even more on what they're already doing instead of preparing for what comes next.

The problem is that **overoptimization is an excellent strategy to win short-term games, yet it is a terrible one for long-term ones.**

Winning long-term games requires resisting overoptimization *even when it looks like a great strategy.*

OPTIMIZATION VS OVER-OPTIMIZATION

A common question I get is, "Luca, *over*-optimization is obviously bad (as implicit in the word *over*), but isn't optimization desirable?"

Yes, but you should seek long-term optimization, not short-term optimization. Or, more precisely: **do optimize for the short term, but never to the measure it endangers the long term.**

That said, it is also possible to over-optimize for the long term. Think about the person who delays gratification so much that they burn out, the entrepreneur who focuses so much on the long term that they lose short-term competitiveness, or the employee who plans their career so much in detail that they miss changes in the labor market.

My personal solution is to spend part of my time caring about the short-term, part of it caring about the medium-term, and part of it improving my long-term future – all of this without ever endangering any of the three time horizons.

This ensures that I build the assets required to achieve my long-term objectives while also preventing risks such as burnout and retaining the flexibility required to adapt to an ever-changing world. Moreover, it ensures that I will have no regrets, regardless of whether I, my business, or my loved ones will cease to exist tomorrow, in a decade, or in fifty years.

Only by balancing the three time horizons, instead of focusing on one exclusively, can you minimize your regrets in the face of uncertainty.

CUMULATIVE RISKS

We have already seen how lying is an example of a risk that's unlikely to materialize over the short term but becomes a massive liability over the long term. If it has, say, a 1% chance of getting discovered, it succeeds 99% of the time. But if you lie once a week, you have a 99.5% chance of getting caught over a decade.

Actions with unlikely risks are excellent tactics but terrible strategies.

This principle is very counterintuitive. If something is a good tactic when done once, it must also be a great tactic to repeat over and over, right?

Wrong.

Time horizons matter, and risks cumulate.

If you want to succeed in the short term, you cannot afford to use tactics that bear a risk of ruin, however small. (Small risks that do not set you back meaningfully in case they materialize are fine.)

Never use short-term evaluations when it comes to estimating risks, especially when those risks cumulate.

CHAPTER SUMMARY

Winning long-term games often requires avoiding what's optimal for the short term.

This won't happen unless you train yourself to make long-term evaluations.

This consists not only of seeing the long-term effects of an action but also of realizing that winning long-term games requires you to take long-term actions *even when it doesn't seem like a good time to do so.* There will always be something more urgent to do – but that urgent thing is unlikely to be what creates a positive inflection point on your life trajectory.

As I wrote in my book "100 Truths You Will Learn Too Late,"

> *"Because the very important does not have a deadline, we have the impression that we can delay it for a few days. It is a huge mistake.*
>
> *Delaying something once opens the door to delaying it forever. If you think about it, the very important never feels urgent."*

Make the important urgent: no one will do it for you.

---

i. Similarly, both short-term players and long-term players play long-term games – after all, we all expect to live until our seventies or eighties. But **short-term players play long-term games as if they were short-term ones,** whereas only long-term players play long-term games embracing their long-term nature.

ii. Not literally and not fully. However, there are indeed many people who adopt similar strategies that cause some early success followed by a large crash – maybe not a crash large enough to become a permanent game over, but large enough to set them back to a worse position than if they had followed a long-term strategy since the beginning.

17

PLAYING ITERATED GAMES

A great way to get yourself to play the long game is to approach every interaction – with your audience, customers, collaborators, partners, etc. – as if it were part of an iterated game. [i]

Do not (just) play it for what you can get in the current interaction. Play to make future ones better.

This includes building trust and collecting information:

– **Building trust** is critical. It could be trust that you are a good person, trust that you understand your interlocutor, or trust that you are competent. Make sure you build all three types of trust.

– **Collecting information** is also critical. It could be information about what the other person likes or is worried about, but also what you are doing wrong, what you could do better, or what the rules of the game are.

When you interact with people, play iterated games: do not just think about what you need but *also* about building trust and collecting information.

SOME EXAMPLES OF PLAYING ITERATED GAMES

– **When performing a task,** focus not only on getting it done this time, but also on learning how to get it done better or faster the next time.

– **When negotiating a deal,** do not focus on getting as much as possible out of it, but instead on getting a fair deal while ensuring that your counterpart keeps wanting to make deals with you.

– **When practicing a skill,** focus not only on improving your skill but also on improving how you practice, so that you can improve faster.

– **When selling a product or service,** market and deliver it in such a way that not only do you make a profit but also improve your reputation.

– **When delegating a task,** do it not just to get something done, but also in such a way that your delegee's skills and engagement increase.

– **When giving negative feedback,** do it in such a way that not only the recipient corrects a mistake but also feels empowered. [ii]

– **When making a decision,** do it not only for its immediate result but also for the future behaviors it makes more or less likely.

CHAPTER SUMMARY

Do not take action for their direct outcome but to make your future actions easier or more effective.

---

i. Readers familiar with the book "Infinite Games" might wonder if this is a similar concept. It is, but only partially: the purpose here is not to keep playing indefinitely but to make success inevitable.
ii. Some principles to help with this include making your feedback as specific as possible, making it actionable (i.e., the recipient shouldn't have to figure out what you meant or what they have to do differently), and building a track record of being competent, reliable, and well-meaning *well before you give the feedback.*

18

LONG-TERM ITERATED GAMES

"The longer view you take, the more apparent it becomes that people who are seemingly competing with each other are actually collaborators."

— *VISAKAN VEERASAMY*

Iterated games become very counterintuitive once you zoom out and consider time scales of a decade or more. For example, over long enough time frames, your competitors are *also* your collaborators. You still compete for a share of the pie, but you also work together to grow the pie.

As a personal anecdote, I began my career as an author believing that other authors in my niche were my competitors. That is true over short time frames, such as "What book will that reader buy next, mine or theirs?" However, over longer time frames, it's more about, "How can I and my competitors educate readers of the value of our niche, so that they buy both my book and theirs?"

As another anecdote, I began my career as a consultant believing that a competitor's failing a project was good for me, for their client might fire them and hire me instead. Later on, I understood that a competitor's failed project also lowers the perceived value of *all* consulting services.

Don't get me wrong! We are still competitors fighting over a share of the pie. But **we should fight in ways that grow the pie and not in ways that shrink it.**

Another area in which iterated games produce counterintuitive results is negotiations. I already mentioned how the short-term approach to negotiations is to get as much as possible out of a single deal, whereas the long-term approach is to get a win-win so that the counterpart is more likely to come to us with another win-win deal.

However, I didn't mention that, over long enough time frames, you want to negotiate win-wins that not only bring results to your suppliers and customers but also grow their long-term assets (skills, relationships, etc.) so that they can produce more or buy more from you.

CHAPTER SUMMARY

Plenty of games are zero-sum over the short term and positive-sum over the long term.

Therefore, playing long-term games as if they were zero-sum often shuns your long-term growth.

Consider which parts of the game you play might shift at least partially to positive-sum over long enough time horizons and play them accordingly.

19

LONG-TERM ASSETS

Here are some examples of long-term assets:

– **Trust** *(of your customers, partners, collaborators, audience, etc.)*

– **Health** *(a healthy body, a healthy mind, non-toxic friends, etc.)*

– **Know-how** *(knowing what needs to be done and how to do it right)*

– **Relationships** *(access to an audience, a particular group of people, etc.)*

– **A body of work** *(that you can sell, that is evidence of your abilities, etc.)*

WHAT ABOUT MONEY?

Money and other financial assets are also forms of long-term assets. That said, particular attention must be given to the fact that money alone won't be sufficient to achieve your objectives *in a sustainable and non-fragile way.* Surprisingly, this includes financial objectives.

If you aim to achieve your financial objectives solely through the accumulation of money and without also accumulating know-how and relationships, your financial capital will be extremely fragile.

WHAT ABOUT TIME?

When we hear that "time is an asset," we often think about the obvious fact that the more time we have, the more things we can do.

But time is an asset also in another important way. The more time we have, the more we can use long-term strategies, which are more effective and reliable than short-term ones.

Hence, it is important to **treat long-term horizons as an asset worth building.**

I stress the word "building." You cannot just decide that your time horizon is going to be long. You must build the conditions that enable it at the level of your finances, your obligations to others, who you work with and their incentives, your health, and so on.

TRUST AND THE LONG TERM

Just like many risks are almost invisible in the short term but become very significant in the long term, so do trust and reputation.

In the short term, the impact of trust looks minimal. If you send a salesy email to your audience, you only see the revenue from the possible sales, not the trust that you might have destroyed in the process.

Of course, this doesn't mean you shouldn't send sales emails. It means you should do it in a way that doesn't reduce their trust in you, because that will harm your long-term prospects more than apparent.

The question is not whether you can progress towards your objective without having built trust. Of course, you can. Instead, the question is whether you can achieve your objective without having built trust, and the answer is: probably not.

20

THE GOOSE AND THE EGGS

You have probably heard Aesop's fable of the Goose and the Golden Egg.[i]

It is about a farmer who discovers that his goose started making golden eggs. Every day, it would lay one. At first, the farmer is grateful. Over time, though, he grows impatient and asks himself, "Why does the goose give me only an egg a day? Why can't it give me all the eggs she has now?" So, he slays the goose and, to his disappointment, discovers that it is empty inside – and now, he cannot get any eggs anymore.

This metaphor explains surprisingly well a common reason that talented and determined people fail to achieve success.

They kill their Goose.

They have some asset – a skill, a product, a reputation, a relationship – and in a bid to get more yield, they squeeze it to the point of damaging its capacity to produce yield.

Never kill your Goose, nor risk it.

SOME WAYS IN WHICH PEOPLE KILL THEIR GOOSE

– An athlete training too hard or taking too many risks and injuring their body *(their Goose)*.

– A solopreneur who writes too many emails to their audience *(their Goose)* selling products instead of providing valuable content. As a result, they teach their audience to ignore their emails.

– A husband or wife who takes their spouse *(their Goose)* for granted and gives them less and less attention to pursue their career, eventually losing them and all the good moments they could have spent together in the future *(the Golden Eggs)*.

– A company that releases a faulty product on the market, breaking the trust of their customers *(their Goose)*.

– A manager who never invests in the development of their team *(their Goose)* and instead squeezes every inch of productivity out of them.

– An investor who invests too much of their money *(their Goose)* on an excessively risky asset to chase marginally higher returns.

As you can see, **the most common reason people kill their Goose or at least put their Goose at risk is because of the desire to get more or to get it faster.**

Ask yourself how you can go faster, but never go faster in a way that puts your Goose at risk.

THERE WILL ALWAYS BE SOMEONE GETTING SUCCESSFUL FASTER THAN YOU

In the first part of this book, I explained how the casino croupier is the only one at the gambling tables with a money-making strategy, yet every day, he sees a few lucky players getting richer than him.

But he would be foolish to abandon his strategy and become a player. Even if he *could* get rich faster, the most likely outcome is that he would get poorer instead.

There will always be someone getting successful faster than you.

That doesn't necessarily mean that they have a better strategy than yours.

Maybe they do, but probably they don't. What matters is not the outcome that their strategy produced for them, but the distribution of outcomes that their strategy is likely to yield.

Never envy someone with a strategy that produces a worse distribution of outcomes than yours, even if, *for them,* it did produce a better outcome.

And never confuse what you *could* achieve with a strategy with what you are likely to achieve.

In fact, **never judge a strategy based on what happens if it works, but judge it based on what happens if it doesn't.**

---

i. While it's a very old fable, I heard the first non-banal application of it in Steven Covey's book, *"The 7 Habits of Highly Effective People,"* which I highly recommend.

21

HIGH- AND LOW-QUALITY SUCCESS

Success can be high- or low-quality, depending on whether it is built on strong or weak foundations.

For example, a sale made by lying to a customer is a form of low-quality success. Conversely, a sale made by honestly answering a customer's questions is a form of high-quality success.

Because of its weak foundations, low-quality success is often temporary and seldom helps with long-term goals. If you rely on luck, luck won't last. If you rely on consuming trust, you will eventually run out of it. And if you rely on bad quality, people will notice.

If your tactic is to overcompensate for a bad product with marketing, you will find yourself with a less profitable structure than your competitors, and that will ultimately hurt your growth. [i]

Moreover, **low-quality success is seldom reproducible.**

Doing more of what brought you low-quality success yields disappointing results. And **imitating someone who achieved low-quality success is unlikely to yield the same success.**

Low-quality success is popular because it takes less time and effort, and it is more efficient and easier to scale. *Only initially, though.*

For example, given two salespeople, the one who lies will have superior first-year sales. But sales will get harder and harder, as he will soon run out of clients to scam and will have to pay a lot in advertising to get more clients. Conversely, the second salesperson will notice that the customers to whom he didn't lie might eventually come back to him and buy again. Some might even refer their friends and colleagues.

High-quality success has a higher potential to scale and sustain over time.

CHAPTER SUMMARY

Only seek or imitate success built on strong foundations.

Success built on weak foundations leads nowhere.[ii]

---

i. For example, going viral with a joke won't help your product sales much (unless your *whole* product is comedy). It will help you sell a few more copies of your product, but there are more effective strategies.
   Similarly, going viral with a controversial tweet won't help your sales much (unless your product is the very topic of the controversy).
   Remember: **the more you optimize for a proxy** (e.g., likes or followers), **the more the proxy decorrelates from the outcome it's supposed to lead to.**

ii. At the net of survivorship bias, obviously. I'm sure there are a few people who enjoyed long-lasting, low-quality success. But most people who achieve low-quality success only have a short-lived moment at the top before falling.
   Again, what matters is not a strategy's potential but the distribution of outcomes it generates *for you.*

22

THE PATH FORWARD

Over the past few pages, we have seen the importance of making long-term evaluations and taking long-term actions even when they seem suboptimal in the short term.

Long-term players do not think, "How can I achieve my goals as fast as possible?" but rather, "How can I increase my chances of achieving them eventually and then sustaining that success?"

The latter question opens up possibilities that don't make sense in the short term but are necessary in the long term, such as building long-term assets (such as trust, skills, relationships, habits, etc.) and playing iterated games, where the focus is not on winning the current game but on making future ones easier.

> Actual shortcuts often appear to be detours. [...] The crowd doesn't understand this. They're always looking for a shortcut that looks like a shortcut.
>
> — *SETH GODIN*

PART IV

DERISK, DERISK, DERISK

There are people who succeed without managing their risks. Yet, if you do not manage your risks, not only are *your* chances of success low (remember survivorship bias?), but your potential will also be limited.

In fact, **just like brakes are not for driving slowly but for enabling driving fast, risk management is not a burden but an enabler of fast growth.**[i]

So, over the next few pages, let's see how you can apply some risk management to your pursuit of success without having to spend too much time and effort on it.

---

i. When done right and reasonably, obviously. Excesses are always bad.

23

LEARNING FROM FAILURE

Studying the successful is a risky path towards success. You might imitate someone who implemented a risky strategy that seldom yields good outcomes or that requires sacrifices you're not willing to make.

A more solid path is to study those who failed despite decent skills and work ethic. This approach is likely to yield good insights into the risks you might face in your journey toward success. Then, you can come up with a strategy that manages those risks.

Make a list of how those smarter than you failed, how those as smart as you failed, and how those less smart than you failed. Smartness is often revised post-hoc, so you don't know yet how smart you truly are.

Then, ask yourself not *whether* you will commit these mistakes but *what* could bring you to do them.

And finally, instead of avoiding the mistake, avoid the conditions that led to that mistake. For example, if "doing drugs" is a common reason for failure, don't ask yourself whether you might do drugs. Ask yourself what could bring you to do drugs and prevent that.

DE-RISK, NOT NO-RISK

Derisking doesn't mean taking zero risks.

In fact, a common reason many people fail to achieve their goals is that they do not take enough risks.

The key is to derisk your long-term goals, not necessarily your short-term bets.

Let me explain.

To achieve most goals, you will have to take a few bets: some ideas that might fail, some projects that might not work out, contacting people who might refuse you, and so on. Those bets are inherently risky. Reducing their risk to zero would be impossible or counterproductive, as it would carry excessive opportunity costs.

However, you should still **ensure that those bets cannot fail** *in a way that would impair your long-term future.* If there's a risk they do, you will have to derisk that.

Moreover, while you can hardly reduce the risk of a bet to zero, usually, there are at least a few actions you can take which, with little work or cost, can significantly increase your odds of success. You should take those de-risking actions.

Now that we've covered the why of derisking, let's move to the how. The first technique we will see is learning from the failures of others.

24

LEARN FROM THE FAILURES OF OTHERS

The second chapter of this book covered 22 common reasons why people fail. I suggest you use that list to perform the following exercise:

1. Pick a long-term goal of yours.
2. Go through the 22 points of the list, and ask yourself what points, if any, might cause you to fail at achieving that goal. Write these down.
3. Ask yourself in what other ways people with the same goal as yours commonly fail. Write those down.
4. Examine all the points you wrote down, and for each, write what you will do to avoid it from causing you to fail.

One tip for you: while doing the previous exercise, avoid thinking you're smarter than others and, therefore, cannot fail. **Even if you are indeed smarter than others, that merely means that you are more likely to do what's required to succeed, but not that you are more likely to do what's required to avoid failure** – ask any investor who was smart enough to pick the right stocks but not wise enough to avoid over-leverage.

BASE RATES, HINDSIGHT, AND NEAR MISSES

We often overestimate how smart we are just because we haven't done anything stupid recently or its consequences haven't materialized yet. For example, 93% of American drivers believe they are better drivers than average – an obvious statistical impossibility. [i]

The culprit is our tendency to rely on hindsight to determine who's a bad driver. If someone drives too fast and crashes, they are a bad driver, but if you drive too fast and didn't crash yet, you feel you are a good driver.

Of course, that doesn't make sense. It is precisely driving too fast that makes you a bad driver, regardless of whether you crashed or got lucky enough and didn't crash yet.

Yes, yes, perhaps you're truly a good driver, and maybe you can drive fast *and* safely. But the chances are that it's precisely your confidence in being a good driver that might make you a bad one – for it might lead to complacency or excessive risk-taking.

The antidote is to look at base rates (if a risk is common, the chances are that it's common for you, too) and near misses (risky situations that could have resulted in an incident but didn't).

For example, if you frequently have to emergency brake to avoid an incident, you are a bad driver – even if you never caused one, because eventually, you will.

---

i. Source: "Are we all less risky and more skillful than our fellow drivers," O. Svenson, 1981.

25

LEARN FROM YOUR FAILURES

A common reason people fail to achieve success is that they do not learn from their failures, or do not learn *enough* from their failures, or learn from their failures but refuse to change their way of doing things based on those learnings.

The root problem is that most of us do not just want to succeed. We want to succeed *in a particular way*. And that is often the seed of failure.

Of course, I'm not saying that you should abandon all your preferences, far from it. But you should realize that preferences have a hefty opportunity cost. Therefore, be deliberate about your priorities.

Of course, you *might* succeed in a particular way. But how likely is it? If the answer is significantly lower than 100%, what can you be flexible on to bring the odds up?

Do not so fixate on a specific way of succeeding so much that it prevents you from learning from experiences showing that a pivot might increase your chances of success.

LEARNING FROM YOUR FAILURES

The only thing worse than not learning from your failures is learning the wrong lessons out of them.

When there are multiple things we could do differently that could improve our outcomes, we often focus on the one we would mind the least doing instead of the most important one.

A good antidote is to acknowledge that **our path toward success is paved with lessons we do not want to learn, and the way forward consists of asking ourselves what unpleasant lessons we have been avoiding.**

Another possibility is to ask ourselves, "If I had done X and Y, I might have avoided failure. But would X and Y have been sufficient to prevent failure fully, or should I have also done something else?" Often, that something else is the true lesson to be learned.

That said, learning from your own failures after they happened is painful. Better to learn from your failures *before* they happen. This is possible with the use of *pre-mortems* and *fishbone diagrams*, which are the topic of the next chapter.

26

LEARN FROM FUTURE FAILURES

You do not have to wait for failure to learn from it.

Ask yourself, "Let's imagine I follow my plan yet fail. What might have gone wrong, and what can I do about it now?"

This simple question, called a *pre-mortem*, is a great way to learn from failure without having to suffer from its consequences.

Of course, this technique has blind spots, but applying it will still get you at least a few good learnings out of it.

To reduce blind spots, you can use an advanced variation of this technique called the *fishbone diagram*. I relegated it to the appendix because describing it takes a few pages, and I didn't want to disrupt the flow of the book. Yet, I encourage you to read and apply it.

If you successfully think about all the ways in which you might fail and others with similar objectives as yours failed, you will bulletproof your strategy and dramatically increase your chance of success.

The next pages contain a few examples.

EXAMPLE #1: A HAPPY RETIREMENT

First of all, let me clarify that I do not optimize my life for retirement. I am still only 35, and as far as I know, I might die tomorrow, at 50, at 75, or at 100 years old. It wouldn't make sense to optimize for a single time horizon. Instead, I try to live my life so that I will die happy regardless of when it will happen.

That said, I often ask myself, "What could cause me to be unhappy assuming I make it to older age, and what can I do about it now?"

Some answers that come to mind are:

– I might have health problems. A healthy lifestyle will prevent that.

– I might feel lonely. Building a solid marriage, nurturing a group of good friends, and having a good relationship with my children will help.

– I might be poor. Getting a good income and investing a significant part of it will help.

I do not think that the chances I will be lonely are very high. Still, I must take them seriously. After all, many elders feel lonely, *including people who didn't think they would feel lonely*. So, do not only prevent the risks you think might happen to you but also look at what happened to others.

Once you come up with a list of possible reasons for failure, work on addressing each to ensure it won't happen to you.

EXAMPLE #2: DELEGATION

As part of my work as a management advisor, I often teach the leaders I consult to pre-mortem the tasks they delegate.

I often tell them,

"Imagine you're about to delegate this task to your subordinate. Let's imagine you delegate them the task, yet they fail. What might have caused the failure? And what are common reasons why people who are delegated similar tasks fail?"

These two questions greatly help my clients to delegate better. Not only do they result in the delegated task being more likely to be completed successfully, but they also help prevent bad delegation from causing failure – something that greatly damages the trust relationship between the subordinate and their manager.

A reminder: in the Appendix, you will find more examples of pre-mortems, including pre-mortems performed using the fishbone diagram method.

A ONE-MINUTE EXERCISE TO DE-RISK YOUR LIFE

1. **Imagine you wake up in a hospital.** What could have been the most likely reason? Is there anything you can do today to prevent that?

2. **Imagine your partner breaks up with you.** What could have been the most likely reason? Is there anything you can do today to prevent that?

3. **Imagine you lose your job.** What could have been the most likely reason? Is there anything you can do today to prevent that?

4. **Imagine you get sued.** What could have been the most likely reason? Is there anything you can do today to prevent that?

5. **Imagine you go on a business trip and receive a missed call from your family in the middle of the night.** What could have been the most likely reason? Is there anything you can do today to prevent that?

(Note: you can find a ready-to-share version of this exercise at Luca-dellanna.com/derisk-exercise)

A ONE-MINUTE EXERCISE TO IMPROVE YOUR LIFE

The previous exercise was about avoiding negative risks.

This exercise is about taking positive risks: risks with limited downside and high upside.

1. **Imagine your relationship with your partner becomes exceptional** *(even if it's already very good)*. What could have been the most likely reason, amongst those in your control? Is there anything you can do today to make that happen?

2. **Imagine that in five years, you doubled your income.** What could have been the most likely reason, amongst those in your control? Is there anything you can do today to make that happen?

3. **Imagine that your project doesn't merely succeed but beats every expectation.** What could have been the most likely reason, amongst those in your control? Is there anything you can do today to make that happen?

Remember that de-risking is not just about preventing the risk that your project ends badly. **De-risking is also about preventing the risk that your project ends up good but not fantastic.**

27

DO NOT ADDRESS EVERY RISK, BUT DO CONSIDER EVERY RISK

The exercises in the previous pages probably produced a long list of possible reasons why you might fail to achieve your long-term goals.

You do not need to address every risk, but you do need to *consider* every risk.

In particular, here are some dos and don'ts:

– **Do** accept a risk of failing at a short-term game, but **only** if that failure does not endanger your long-term strategy. *For example, it is okay for a project to fail, but not in a way that endangers your reputation.*

– **Do not** underestimate base rates. If a risk is a frequent cause of failure for others, it is very likely to be a major risk for you too, even if you feel immune to it.

– **Do** consider the cumulative nature of risks with a low chance of happening next year but a high chance of occurring over the next decade.

– **Do not** address every risk perfectly: some are too expensive to nullify.

– **Do,** for every risk, ask yourself: is there at least an imperfect action I can take to reduce its chances of occurring? Apply the 80/20 rule.

– **Do not, under any circumstance,** accept a risk that might lower your chances of succeeding *eventually* below 99%. *(See the chapter after the next one, "Inevitability.")*

28

WHEN TO STICK WITH A PROJECT AND WHEN TO ABANDON IT

Here are two common mistakes people make:

1. Abandoning a project too early.
2. Sticking with a project for too long.

Given a single project, it is hard to know whether you're committing one of these two mistakes. However, you can look at patterns in your behavior across projects, such as:

– **You *always* drop projects early,** never giving them a proper chance and never iterating at least once on them.

– **You *never* drop projects voluntarily,** always spending time and effort on them even after it would have been time to move on.

– **You keep procrastinating on key to-do items in your project,** which indefinitely delays *meaningful* progress.

Those three red flags point to some limiting belief, psychological obstacle, or emotional association that will prevent you from succeeding until you address it. Depending on which applies to you, you should consider adjusting your approach in the opposite direction more than it seems instinctive to you.

Note: the Appendix chapter "Managing Bets" contains a more detailed discussion of this topic.

29

INEVITABILITY

*You only get one life.
Why spend it pursuing paths that might not work out?*

Short-term strategies *can* work.

If enough people try them, there will be many winners. So, such strategies look impressive and worth imitating.

But you only have one life. **You shouldn't be satisfied with a strategy that *might* work.**

You want to adapt your strategy so that your success is *inevitable*.

Is this possible, though?

Not for all types of success, obviously. For example, no strategy can guarantee to become the #1 in the world at something, because all it takes is a second person implementing the same strategy to make it a coin toss.

But for most types of success, you can have a strategy that stacks the odds of success in your favor, making your success almost inevitable. Or, at the very least, you can adapt your current strategy by asking yourself, "How can I make my success more inevitable?"

HOW TO INCREASE INEVITABILITY

Do not be satisfied with a chance of success. Instead, continuously ask yourself, "How can I increase my chances of success until almost certainty?"

This usually means doing two things. The first one is to play short-term games not to win them but to advance towards your long-term objectives. For example, do projects not to make the most money out of them but to learn skills, test hypotheses, and build trust and an audience. If you do so, each project will grow the long-term assets that will eventually make your success almost inevitable.

The second thing to do to increase inevitability is to take more bets than apparently necessary, work on more projects than apparently necessary, meet more people than apparently necessary, and so on. The more you do this, the higher the chance that at least one of them will represent a major step forward towards success.

The next chapter is about how to do that.

30

INCREASE YOUR LUCK

Most successful people are talented and/or hard-working. That said, they also got lucky.

This does not mean that they didn't deserve their success. First of all, it's not like they didn't work hard. Moreover, if they got lucky, it's often because they appropriately exposed themselves to chance.

The lesson is that **relying only on talent and hard work might not be enough. You must also increase your luck – or, more precisely, its surface area.** This roughly means two things:

1. You should expose yourself to sources of upside: meeting people, showing your work, trying things that might not work, etc. Not doing this will severely limit your potential.

2. Doing the above might not be sufficient unless you do it enough times to guarantee that it's almost certain that at least one will bring you the success you seek within your relevant time horizon. Not doing this means you might do everything right and still fail.

The second point is of paramount importance yet often neglected.

PRACTICAL APPLICATIONS

If you are an author, one book might suffice to achieve success, but maybe it will take ten. You must acknowledge the possibility. So, work on your books fast enough so that you get to write ten before it's too late.

Of course, you cannot just publish a bad book. You must work on it long enough for it to be good enough to have a decent chance at succeeding. *(More on this in the appendix chapter, "Managing Bets.")* Still. If you work on it too slowly so that you can publish at most one or two within your lifetime, you're limiting your chances of success.

As another example, if you are an entrepreneur, you might achieve success with your first product, but maybe it will take ten. Adjust your processes and spending to increase both your launch cadence and financial runway so that you get to take those ten bets. Also, play the long game. Do not over-promise what the first product does: in case of failure, you will break the trust early investors and adopters put in you. Instead, communicate transparently in such a way that even if you fail, you will have strengthened the relationships that will make the second launch more likely to succeed.

Do not play short-term games hoping to succeed with your first attempt. Instead, play the long game (which, in this case, doesn't mean taking forever to launch but rather taking many bets).

31

THE PATH FORWARD

The third and fourth parts of this book guided you in maximizing your chances of achieving any given long-term goal.

You learned about the importance of learning from the mistakes of others before they become your mistakes, and of learning from your mistakes before you commit them (thanks to *pre-mortems*).

The fifth and final part of this book is about managing multiple goals. For example, how do you achieve your professional objectives while also achieving your personal and spiritual ones?

PART V

HOLISTIC SUCCESS

Just like you cannot optimize short-term games in a vacuum but must instead optimize them for their effect on the long game, **you cannot optimize for a long-term goal in a vacuum but must optimize it for its effect on your whole life.**

Let's say that one of your long-term goals is to become a CEO. You cannot fully optimize for that goal unless it's the only thing you want and will want out of your life. People who become CEOs by working so hard that they destroy their health and marriage succeed yet still fail.

If you optimize your long-term goals in a vacuum, you might achieve them in a way that won't matter, because it will have precluded your other eventual goals.

So, how do you optimize your long-term goals while considering their mutual impact? This fifth and final part of this book will help you do precisely that.

32

RACES TO THE BOTTOM

Life is full of races to the bottom: some careers, businesses, communities, and activities that eventually became a competition for who's willing to sacrifice more.

During the first years, skill and a decent work ethic are enough to get ahead. This lures many into believing they have an easy shot at winning.

However, as the race progresses, competition becomes fiercer. Skill and a decent work ethic aren't enough anymore. Keeping up requires an unreasonable work ethic, and getting ahead demands reckless risk-taking.

Participants with a narrow vision for success let their eagerness to win set their boundaries. As a result, they often find themselves with miserable lives – they either sacrificed too much or took too much risk and lost.

Conversely, participants with a broad vision for success are more eager to have a full life than to win any race to the bottom. As a result, they set ambitious objectives for all important parts of their life.

Then, they use these objectives to set their boundaries – what they are not willing to risk and sacrifice. And finally, they use these boundaries to decide how to compete in races to the bottom and to what point.

These are the real winners: even if they do not get #1, they get out of the race more than they risked and sacrificed. Because they choose the conditions at which to compete, they end up with a good bargain.

Be careful of any career, community, or hobby you participate in. Are they races to the bottom? Do they have the potential to become such?

Races to the bottom are tricky because, initially, when your competition isn't very good and a bit of effort is sufficient to win them, they look worth participating in. But then, they get increasingly difficult and soon require excessive sacrifices. So, it's important to ask ourselves to which point it makes sense to participate in them. Not *if*, but to which point.

WHICH RACES ARE TO THE BOTTOM?

A race to the bottom is a race where the winner is the person who's willing to take more risks and/or make more sacrifices.

In theory, races where all participants cannot or do not want to make excessive sacrifices are not races to the bottom. An example would be career progression in a company where no one works beyond 5 p.m.

However, there is no way to guarantee that participants do not make excessive sacrifices. In the previous example, no one can prevent an employee from taking work home or spending the evenings practicing some skill that will be helpful to get promoted.

Therefore, **it is the size of a race that determines whether it is to the bottom.** The smaller the race, the less likely that amongst its participants, there will be someone willing to make excessive sacrifices.

In contrast, a large race, or one with a large enough prize, is more likely to attract at least one participant aggressive enough to turn it into a race to the bottom.

The problem with races to the bottom is that the larger the race, the larger the prize and thus the temptation to participate in it, but the difficulty and sacrifices required to win scale much faster than the prize. Hence, they are less worthwhile to participate in than apparent.

AVOIDING RACES TO THE BOTTOM

Avoiding races altogether is very hard, if not impossible. After all, in our lives, we are unwilling participants in many races: school, work, and finding a partner are all competitions, even if we do not want them to be.

The solution is to be extremely clear with our boundaries and only participate in races to the bottom to the extent our boundaries allow. For example, a career is a race to the bottom, but a career where you never work beyond 5 PM isn't. Similarly, a career in sales can be a race to the moral bottom, but a career in sales done with integrity isn't.

Again, note that **this is not an invitation to minimize your ambitions. Rather, it is an invitation to maximize them.** Make a list of everything you want out of life, in all its spheres: professional, social, spiritual, fun, etc. Then, ask yourself which boundaries you will need to have to achieve all your ambitions. Only afterward, figure out which races you should compete in and to what point.

If you do this exercise properly, you might achieve more in life than you might ever achieve if you focus on winning a single race to the bottom.

WINNING RACES TO THE BOTTOM

You can reliably win a race to the bottom only if you do not need to get #1 for it to have a net positive effect on your life – because no strategy can reproducibly get you #1 in a race to the bottom.

The previous paragraph might raise objections such as, "But Luca, obviously a mix of hard work and a great strategy can make you #1!"

Yes, but let's not confuse "winning" with "winning reproducibly." Of course, barring cheating, everyone who wins a competition is a worthy winner. And, of course, they wouldn't have won without hard work. But that doesn't mean that talent, hard work, and a great strategy can guarantee winning. At most, they guarantee *a chance* of winning.

Let me make a concrete example. Leo Messi's Argentina won the 2022 World Cup (soccer). Did they deserve it? Totally. Were they the best team? Possibly. Were they guaranteed to win? Not at all. Betting companies gave them less than 50% odds. Why? Because, at a large competition such as the World Cup, there are enough competitors that even the best one has only small odds.

In large competitions, the sheer number of competitors means there will be more than one competitor talented and hard-working enough to have a decent shot at winning. Therefore, there is no reproducible strategy for winning large competitions. So, you shouldn't enter any non-trivial competition that wouldn't be good for you even if you didn't win it.

Winning Long-Term Games

SMALLER COMPETITIONS

Conversely, small competitions do allow reproducible success strategies.

Because they contain a smaller group of participants, the chances of competing against someone very talented and hard-working are smaller. It is easier to become the best chess player in your town than in your country.

In small competitions, you can outwork or outsmart your competitors without having to incur excessive risks and sacrifices.

If you do have bad luck and encounter a fierce competitor, it will probably be only one or two of them. You will still be able to reproducibly be #2 or #3.

And if you really want to be #1, because it's a small competition, you can always move or pivot to another small competition. If being the best chess player in your town is impossible because a grandmaster happened to be born down the street, you can always pivot to another game.

But what if your only dream is to become the greatest chess player in your country? In this case, you must acknowledge that it is going to be a race to the bottom, that you will have to sacrifice more than you might be comfortable with, and that you will end up with, at most, a chance at winning.

Then, of course, the choice of whether to participate is yours.

33

SPILLOVERS

There are plenty of successful yet unhappy people.

Sometimes, the success they sought doesn't taste as nice as they expected. But more often, it's because they discovered that their pursuit of success had more "negative spillovers" on the rest of their life than they expected.

Not only should your strategy to achieve success be sustainable (so that you can pursue it long enough to guarantee success), **but it should also be devoid of major negative spillovers over other areas of your life.**

For example, avoid any strategy that requires you to endanger your health or marriage. It's not worth it. More in general, avoid any strategy to achieve a given goal that's incompatible with your other goals.

If you discover that no strategy fits this criterion, you might have incompatible goals. If so, you will have to compromise on your goals or set more conservative ones. This is not a choice: either you compromise, or life will, letting you achieve some of your goals but not others.

34
COMPARISONS AND THE PARETO FRONTIER

Every time I participate in a High School reunion, I get a choice on how I compare myself to others.

One possibility is to notice that, amongst my former classmates, there is at least one who earns more than me, at least one who has more free time than me, and so on.

Another possibility is to notice that, amongst my former classmates who make at least as much money as me, I'm the one with the most free time. And amongst those who have at least as much free time as me, I'm the one who makes the most money.

Learning to see success using this lens is highly beneficial. For example, do you want to be the most successful you can be, or do you want to be the most successful you can be while always having dinner with your family? Then, you shouldn't compare yourself with anyone who doesn't also spend all dinners with their family.

Never compare yourself with someone having different boundaries or optimizing for different objectives or for a shorter time horizon. Doing so leads to unhappiness and/or to making counterproductive decisions.

THE PARETO FRONTIER

In the previous page, I presented two ways to compare yourself to others.

1) "There is someone who earns more than me and someone with more free time than me."

2) "Amongst those who earn as much as me, I have the most free time, and amongst those with as much free time as me, I earn the most."

The second type of evaluation is called the *Pareto Frontier*, taking the name from the Italian mathematician Vilfredo Pareto (the same one who invented the *Pareto Rule*, also called the *"80/20 rule"* – 20% of your customers are responsible for 80% of your problems, and so on.)

In particular, I am at the Pareto Frontier if, given two metrics, A and B, among everyone who has at least as much A as me, I have the most B, and among everyone who has at least as much B as me, I have the most A.

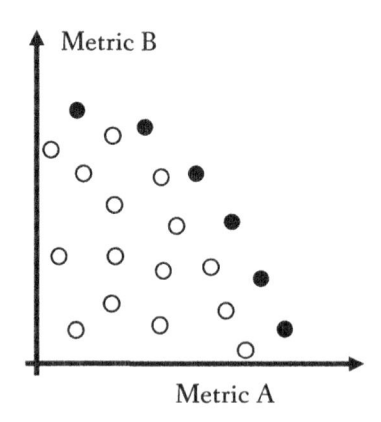

All the black dots are on the Pareto Frontier for metrics A and B

COMPARING OPTIONS

The previous chapter began with a comparison between people, but the Pareto Frontier is also useful to compare options.

For example, without knowing about the Pareto Frontier, you might compare jobs asking yourself which one is the highest paying. Instead, using the Pareto Frontier, you might ask yourself better questions, such as, what's the highest-paying job amongst those that enable you to spend enough time with your family?

The Pareto Frontier isn't a revolutionary concept – many of us already make decisions with a similar mental process. However, giving it a name and making it explicit is useful because it shows that picking a job that's not the highest paying is not necessarily a lazy or suboptimal choice.

If it is at the Pareto Frontier of what matters to you, it is an ambitious and optimal choice.

THE PARETO FRONTIER AND WINNING LONG-TERM GAMES

Single-metric comparisons such as "who earns more" are toxic because they lead to feelings of inferiority and/or races to the bottom.

Conversely, comparing yourself to others using multi-metric comparisons such as the Pareto Frontier is a relatively healthy way to ask yourself whether you're being ambitious enough. If you are at the Pareto Frontier of what matters to you, you're probably doing fine (as long as you being there isn't the result of short-term optimization). Conversely, if you are far from your Pareto Frontier, you might have been too lazy or conservative.

But perhaps more importantly, defining success in terms of Pareto frontiers helps you avoid the temptation to follow those who take excessive risks or make sacrifices you're not willing to take.

Instead of aiming to be the most successful, aim to be the most successful amongst those who play long-term games and aren't willing to take excessive risks or sacrifices.

Your distribution of outcomes will improve.

CHAPTER SUMMARY

You are at the Pareto Frontier if, given two metrics A and B that matter to you, amongst those who have at least enough A as you, you are the one with the most B, and amongst those who have at least enough B as you, you are the one with the most A.

The Pareto Frontier is a great way to compare options, but also a healthy way to compare yourself to others.

Most importantly, it prevents you from comparing yourself with those with a shorter time horizon than yours – a comparison that's toxic because it sets you up for failure (you cannot compete with short-term optimizers over the short term[i]) and tempts you into abandoning good long-term strategies in favor of bad short-term ones.

---

i. I mean, obviously, you *can* compete, but you most probably won't win.
    You will not do badly because good long-term strategies never do poorly, but survivorship bias almost guarantees that there will be at least a few short-term players who will beat you – at least over short time horizons.

35

CHOOSE REPRODUCIBLE OBJECTIVES

Long-term strategies have amazing potential and can help you reliably achieve your life goals, but they aren't magical. They cannot help you reliably achieve objectives that cannot be achieved reproducibly.

For example, becoming #1 in the world at something is not reproducible, because all it takes is someone else applying the same strategy as yours, at which point it almost becomes a coin toss.

This concept is counterintuitive because of our assumption that if a competition involves skill, then becoming the most skilled guarantees victory. This is seldom true. Obviously, skill still matters and is table stakes. However, luck and other considerations still play a large role.

Think about chess. In appearance, chess is the quintessential skill game, as it includes no dice or other random elements. Yet, if two players of similar skill levels face each other and play a series of games, the more skilled player will only win some of them. In fact, in the last Chess World Championship Finals *(2023, Ding vs Nepomniachtchi)*, the winning player only won 57% of the games, excluding draws. This means there is a meaningful chance that the losing player was more skilled than the winner!

We often mistakenly believe that strategies depend on luck to the extent they relate to events we have little control over. But this is wrong – for example, there are good investing strategies to bet on stocks over which we have no control, whereas chess games where we have full control over our moves can still be a coin toss if we face an adversary of similar skill.

Instead, what determines whether a strategy depends on luck is its structure and how many winners there can be. Investing is luck-dependent only if we bet so aggressively that we can only afford a few wrong bets before accumulating excessive losses. And winning an award is more luck-dependent the more limited the number of winners.

Only goals that allow enough winners and can be played many times are reproducible.

Choose reproducible goals. Or, at least, acknowledge that you chose non-reproducible ones and that, therefore, no matter your talent and determination, you have at most a *chance* at achieving them, but no guarantee.

CHAPTER SUMMARY

No strategy can guarantee success for goals that only allow a limited number of winners or a limited number of trials.

The first step to reproducible success is to choose reproducible goals.

36

THE 1% LIFE

When I was a kid, I thought I had no chance to get a great wife. After all, there were plenty of people fitter than me, plenty more charismatic than me, plenty wealthier than me, and so on.

Then, one day, a friend told me: "Luca, if you don't get overweight, you will be in the top 30% of the population by physique. If you get a decent job, you will get in the top 30% by wealth. If you aren't crazy and can sustain a normal conversation cracking a joke or two, you will be in the top 30% by interpersonal skills. And if you manage to do all three at the same time, you will be in the top 10% of bachelors, perhaps even top 5%."

It turns out that **the bar is not that high if you look at the aggregate instead of single attributes.**

If one of your goals is, say, to live a top 1% life – a life better than 99% of your fellow compatriots – you do not need to be in the top 1% by wealth or health to get there. Similarly, if you want to be, say, a top 1% professional, you can probably realize that you can achieve that by being in the top 20% by skills, top 20% by work ethics, and very good at not making major mistakes.

BUT IS TOP 1% REALLY ACHIEVABLE?

I do believe that, barring rare debilitating conditions, a top 1% life is really achievable – especially if you consider top-1% in the context of the Pareto Frontier. Again, not a top-1% income, but a top-1% life.

I might be wrong, and maybe what's truly achievable for most readers of this book is top 2%, or some other percentage. That's not the point.

The point is that **the path toward excellence and a great life involves going broad** *and* **narrow.**

We often get the opposite impression because the excellent are often very good at a particular skill. But this often hides that, first and foremost, they are also much better than average at plenty of other skills, and that without such broad proficiency, their narrow excellence would have been near useless.

Take any NBA star with excellent offensive skills, like Ray Allen or Steph Curry. Yes, their offensive skills are extraordinary. But their defensive skills are also above average! If you think about it, there are plenty of basketball players who are excellent at some particular skill but never make it to the pros because of their lack of some other indispensable skill.

Narrow excellence requires broad excellence to bring good outcomes.

Hence, my encouragement is to go broader before you go narrower.

This doesn't mean to spread yourself too thin. It means to realize that **if you go narrow and don't** *also* **go broad, going narrow won't matter.**

Think about your life as a whole and try to succeed in all its aspects that matter to you significantly – family, career, health, wealth, etc. Otherwise, succeeding in one will feel like it didn't matter.

CHAPTER SUMMARY

To be in the top-1% at something, you don't have to be top-1% at all its components.

Prioritize going broad over going narrow. If you go narrow but don't also go broad, having gone narrow won't have mattered.

37

HAPPINESS RULES

> "What has to happen in order for you to feel good? Do you have to have someone hug you, kiss you, make love to you? Must you make a million dollars? [...] If you make [that], the million dollars doesn't give you any pleasure. It's your rule that says, "When I hit this mark, I'll give myself permission to feel good.
>
> — *TONY ROBBINS*

What needs to happen for you to feel happy?

Not the fleeting kind of happiness that's followed by hollowness, but the real kind of happiness, the one that warms your heart and makes you feel proud of your choices.

What rules of yours determine when you give yourself permission to be happy?

Unless you know your happiness rules, your strategy will be misguided.

38

IT'S CLOSER THAN WE THINK

In 2023, the judges of the prestigious Gilbert et Gaillard international wine competition awarded the gold medal to a $2.70 supermarket wine they deemed "exceptional" (they got tricked by a fake label).

A bottle of good wine is cheap. It is a bottle of good wine with an expensive label that's expensive.

Going out is cheap. It's going out to an expensive place that's expensive.

These might very well be platitudes, but they're *ignored* platitudes.

"90% of a millionaire lifestyle is already available to you," wrote Mark Baker in his *"No Money Millionaire."*

I think he's right. I genuinely feel I live like a millionaire without being one – perhaps precisely because not having "becoming a millionaire" as one of my life goals is so freeing. It enables me to have more time, to work on the projects I like, to live close to my parents even though it's not the most conducive city for business, and, in general, it makes all other life goals so much easier to attain.

("The average of your top five friends influences your income expenses," I say.)

I'm not advocating for frugality here. Instead, I'm suggesting that **there's a high cost of opportunity in wanting more than you need** in one area of your life because it will make it harder to attain what you need in other areas of your life.

Nor am I saying to lower your ambitions. Instead, I'm saying to raise them! Aim for what you need, not in a single area of your life but in all of them!

This might require some introspection about what you really need – and the ability to resist moving the goalposts once you achieve that.

> "Remember when you wanted what you have now?"
>
> — *KATELYN GLEASON (ELIGIBLE CEO)*

CHAPTER SUMMARY

There is a high cost of opportunity in wanting more than you need.

Be ambitious and try to achieve more than you need, but only when it doesn't come at the cost of something else you need in another area of your life.

> "It's insane to risk what you have and need for something you don't really need."
>
> — *WARREN BUFFET*

CONCLUSIONS

IN PART I OF THIS BOOK,

We have seen that the key to winning long-term games is to stop playing them as a succession of *separate* short-term games. Instead, play short-term games not to win them but to increase your chances of winning the long-term game.

We have also seen that you *can* win long-term games without addressing common causes of failure, but the chances are that you won't. To have a good chance of winning long-term games, you must be aware of common sources of failure and proactively do something about them.

Then, we went through the three components of good long-term strategies: they are sustainable, constructive, and inevitable.

Finally, we have seen that if you optimize each component of a strategy individually, you won't have an optimal strategy. Instead, you should follow an iterative approach and optimize for the distribution of outcomes.

IN PART II OF THIS BOOK,

We have seen how long-term strategies are truly superior to short-term ones.

If it seems otherwise, it is either because of survivorship bias or because we focus on short-term performance. *Of course*, short-term strategies deliver better short-term performance. But if what matters to you is long-term performance, make long-term evaluations.

Remember the image below, from the chapter on survivorship bias. Always ask yourself, does my strategy look more like Alice's or Bob's?

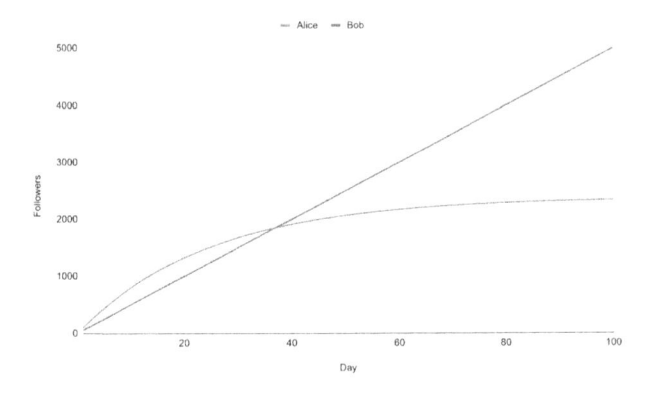

Of course, you also want to ensure you don't have a bad long-term strategy that begins like Bob's but ends up like Alice's. You still need to take effective action, and you still need to do it with urgency, trying to succeed as fast as possible – but only as fast *as long-term evaluations allow it*. In other words, only as fast as possible without compromising your long-term assets or your chances of success.

IN PART III OF THIS BOOK,

We have seen the importance of not merely considering the long term but also leveraging it.

We discussed the importance of playing iterated games, which you play not to maximize what you get out of the current interaction but to make the next one better.

We also saw that short-term games are about getting a larger share of the pie, whereas long-term games are also about growing the pie.

We discussed the importance of building long-term assets (such as skills, habits, and trust) and of doing so *even when it doesn't look like a good time, because it never will be a good time*. If you never build them, you will never grow beyond an early plateau.

We saw how many talented and determined people fail to achieve success because they kill their Goose. They have some asset (a skill, a product, a reputation, a relationship), and in a bid to get more yield, they squeeze it to the point of damaging its capacity to produce yield.

Finally, we have seen the importance of only seeking success solid enough to act as an effective foundation for your long-term goals.

IN PART IV OF THIS BOOK,

We have seen the importance of derisking.

Just like brakes are not to drive slowly but to enable driving fast, risk management is not a burden but an enabler of fast growth.

Much of derisking is about learning what you need to learn before you get hurt. That means learning from the failures of others and preempting the possible ways in which you might fail – for example, using pre-mortems and fish diagrams.

We have also seen that you shouldn't be satisfied with a strategy for your long-term goals that might work, but you should look for a strategy that cannot fail. Failure is acceptable for projects but not for your life goals.

FINALLY, IN PART V OF THIS BOOK,

We discussed holistic success.

We have seen the importance of avoiding races to the bottom – competitions where even winners lose. Or, at the very least, to only enter them at your conditions and never compromise your boundaries *(as long as they are reasonable, of course)*.

We have also learned about the Pareto Frontier and the opportunity to evaluate your life in a way that considers all trade-offs. And the importance of never comparing yourself against people with a shorter time horizon than yours or with narrower goals.

I concluded the book with an invitation to think about what your happiness rules are and to avoid seeking more than you need *when doing so would endanger your other life goals.*

THE END?

This marks the end of this book. I hope it's been as helpful to you as it's been helpful to everyone with whom I shared its early drafts.

That's not the end, though.

First of all, at the very end of this manuscript, there is **an appendix** that digs deeper into a few specific use cases – for example, what if you are an investor or an employee?

Moreover, I expect to write additional essays about Winning Long-Term Games over the next few months. To receive them, subscribe to my mailing list at **Luca-Dellanna.com/newsletter**. In alignment with the spirit of this book, I write emails that reward rather than consume my audience's attention.

ANY QUESTIONS?

Finally, if you have any questions, feel free to send me an email at **Luca@Luca-Dellanna.com**. I read all replies personally.

And if you need professional support on risk management or otherwise applying the contents of your book to your life or company, feel free to reach out to me – that's what I do for work.

Thank you for having read this book, and please share about it!

And if you have enjoyed it, please leave a review on Amazon or Goodreads!

ABOUT THE AUTHOR
LUCA DELLANNA

Luca has over ten years of experience advising senior leaders on risk-, operations-, and people- management.

For some clients, he acts as an on-demand advisor to provide expertise on the topics of his competence. For others, he conducts short workshops to efficiently increase the managerial capabilities of their leaders. Sometimes, he also conducts *short* on-the-field consulting engagements and benchmark audits.

In addition to his advisory activity, Luca is an external lecturer at a few universities in Italy and the UK, and frequently speaks at conferences and internal company events. Luca is also the author of ten books and an independent economics, behavioral sciences, and epidemiology researcher having presented at large conferences and won international research grants.

An automotive engineer by training, after having led large teams and consulted for large multinationals, in 2015, Luca quit his corporate job to become an independent advisor, researcher, and author. After living in Spain, Germany, and Singapore, he moved back to his hometown of Turin (Italy), where he currently lives with his wife Wenlin and dog Didi.

Luca writes regularly on Twitter (**@DellAnnaLuca**). You can visit his website at **Luca-dellanna.com**. You can also contact him at **Luca@luca-dellanna.com** *(he reads all emails personally)*.

In the following pages, you can find a brief overview of Luca's other books. You can support him by recommending this book to your friends or colleagues and leaving a review on Amazon.

𝕏 x.com/DellAnnaLuca
in linkedin.com/in/dellannaluca
▶ youtube.com/LucaDellannaChannel

ALSO BY LUCA DELLANNA

Winning Long-Term Games (2024)

Managing Hybrid and Remote Teams, 2nd ed. (2024)

Ergodicity: How Irreversible Outcomes Affect Long-term Performance in Work, Investing, Relationships, Sport, and Beyond, 3rd ed. (2023)

The Employee Engagement Handbook (2023)

The Pandemic Guidebook (2022)

100 Truths You Will Learn Too Late, 3rd ed. (2021)

Teams Are Adaptive Systems (2020)

The Control Heuristic, 2nd ed. (2020)

The Power of Adaptation (2018)

The World Through a Magnifying Glass, 2nd ed. (2018)

ERGODICITY

How Irreversible Outcomes Affect Long-term Performance in Work, Investing, Relationships, Sport, and Beyond (3rd ed.)

"This is one of the most important books I've read, period. It's short, articulate, and expansive on a singular subject matter — ergodicity, which is really the key ingredient to success in life, marriage, business, family, happiness, health, etc."

— *BLAKE JANOVER, JANOVER INC. CEO*

"A great book for those who quickly want to familiarize themselves with the concept of ergodicity. The author goes to great lengths to explain the concept in easily understandable terms. Highly recommended!"

—*AUKE HUNNEMAN*

BEST PRACTICES FOR OPERATIONAL EXCELLENCE (3ᴿᴰ ED.)

"I'm a huge fan of High Output Management and Setting the Table [...] Luca's Best Practices for Operational Excellence took my management to the next level. It's been almost a month since I started implementing the principles, but I can already say that I've noticed a significant improvement in my company's morale [...] That feels amazing."

— *MOLSON HART, VIAHART CEO*

THE CONTROL HEURISTIC: THE NATURE OF HUMAN BEHAVIOR (2ND ED.)

"This book is like a magnificent suspension bridge, linking the science of the human brain to the practical craft of applying it in everyday life. I loved it."

— RORY SUTHERLAND

"A SUPERB book [...] by one of the profound thinkers in our field [behavioral economics]."

— MICHAL G. BARTLETT

"Luca's book was so helpful to my work. Opened my eyes up to some more reasons why change is so hard."

— CHRIS MURMAN

MANAGING HYBRID AND REMOTE TEAMS (2ND ED.)

"Lots of specific and practical advice! Even experienced managers should find each chapter hugely valuable for reassessing their performance in each of the areas.

— *GABY LLOYD*

"Packed full of useful information. Luca takes the maddeningly difficult subject of managing a team and breaks it down into actionable activities. The sections on Clarity and Feedback are particularly strong, providing a way of viewing management as a nurturing and human activity.

— *DANIEL WEBB*

"Thought-provoking."

— *CARL BROWN*

100 TRUTHS YOU WILL LEARN TOO LATE (3RD ED.)

"I am amazed at Luca Dellanna's ability to observe, compile, and articulate 99 very actionable life principles here. Each chapter describes the rule in a way that makes you think and then summarizes the Action. It's filled with DEEP insights yet VERY readable."

— *THERESIA TANZIL*

"Absolutely brilliant. You might have grasped some of these concepts before, but having them structured and in writing makes all the difference [...] I will surely recommend it to friends and co-workers."

— *ALBERTO PISANELLO*

"A very thoughtful piece of writing, deep and wiring!"

— *DAVID KREJCA*

THE WORLD THROUGH A MAGNIFYING GLASS (2ND ED.)

"Thank you for helping me understand! My son was recently diagnosed, and I needed to be able to understand how he views the world. Why would certain things overwhelm him and cause so much anxiety and pain. This book made it so clear and easy to understand."

— *GEIGER T.*

Probably one of the best works I have read on autism (I have read a few), and it's surprising how realistically he depicts the condition."

— *MANEL VILAR*

"Loved The World Through a Magnifying Glass – this analogy NAILS IT."

— *EMERSON SPARTZ, NYT BESTSELLER AUTHOR*

APPENDIX

The appendix contains additional chapters that deepen some of the topics explored over the previous hundred pages.

The chapters **"Fishbone Diagrams," "Managing Bets," "Committing to The Long Term While Retaining Flexibility,"** and **"Learning and Adaptation"** complement Part 4, "Derisk, derisk, derisk."

The chapters **"Mixed Feelings"** and **"Don't Try to Be Too Smart"** complement the list of 22 common reasons people might fail.

After that, the chapter **"Common goals and how to make them more reproducible"** provides a few examples of how to put into practice the learnings of this book.

Finally, you might also benefit from joining my mailing list at **Luca-Dellanna.com/newsletter**, where I plan to publish a few additional essays complementing this book.

39

FISHBONE DIAGRAMS

While pre-mortems are an extremely powerful tool, they are by no means sufficient to come up with a comprehensive list of what could go wrong. You might have blind spots or simply forget about something important.

Here is a tool to help you: *fishbone diagrams*. They are traditionally used in manufacturing for root-cause analysis, but I also use them with my clients to derisk their projects and ventures.

The picture below is an example. It is a diagram that looks like a fishbone (hence the name) and is read from right to left. It begins with a failure (the "fish head," in this case a "my book didn't become a best-seller") and continues with four possible categories of causes (the four "main bones"), which in turn branch out in many possible root causes.

See the following diagram.

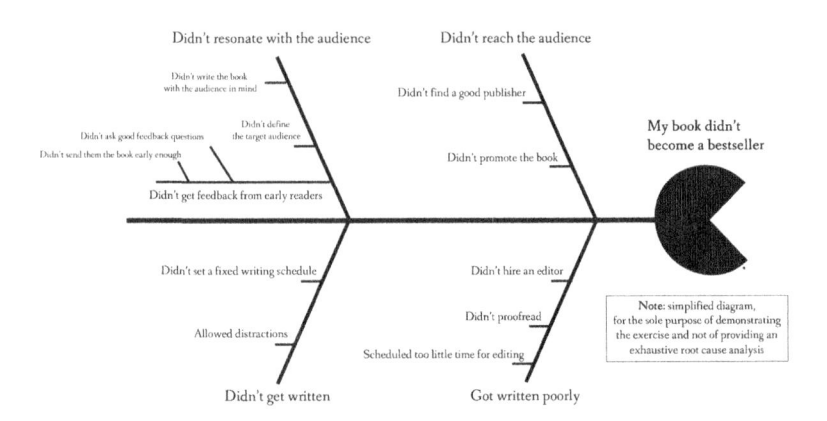

*An example of a fishbone diagram. A larger image is available at **Luca-Dellanna.com/fishbone***

Traditionally, fishbone diagrams are used for post-mortems. For example, if your latest marketing campaign didn't work, you might draw a fishbone diagram to figure out what might have caused the problem.

Of course, it is possible to figure out root causes without using fishbone diagrams. However, drawing one decreases the chances of leaving out something important.

That said, I find **fishbone diagrams very useful for *pre*-mortems.** Of course, you could conduct effective pre-mortems without drawing a fishbone diagram. But drawing one will make them even more comprehensive and might even reveal some blind spots of yours.

In the next pages, you will find a few examples of fishbone diagrams applied to some common life goals.

Before that, a few tips for effective fishbone diagrams:

1. Ask yourself both what could fail *and* how others failed in related situations.

2. Write down any possibility, no matter how unlikely. You don't have to address every risk, but you must *consider* every risk.
3. The largest bones should be as mutually exclusive and collectively exhaustive as possible.
4. Always ask yourself multiple times, "What else?"

TWO EXAMPLES OF FISHBONE DIAGRAMS

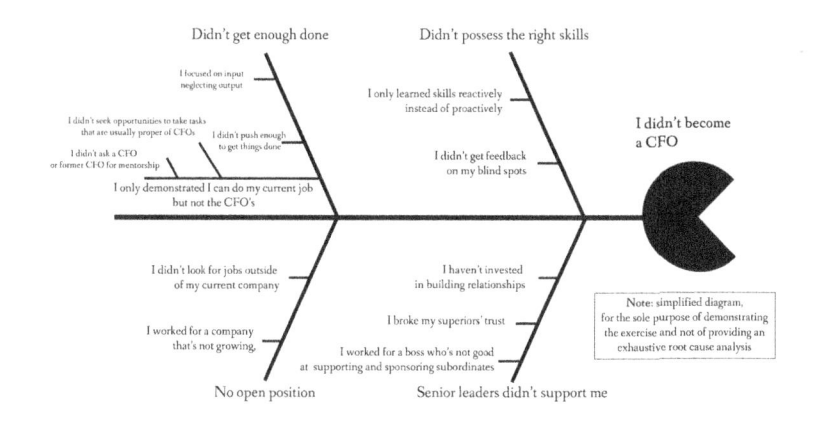

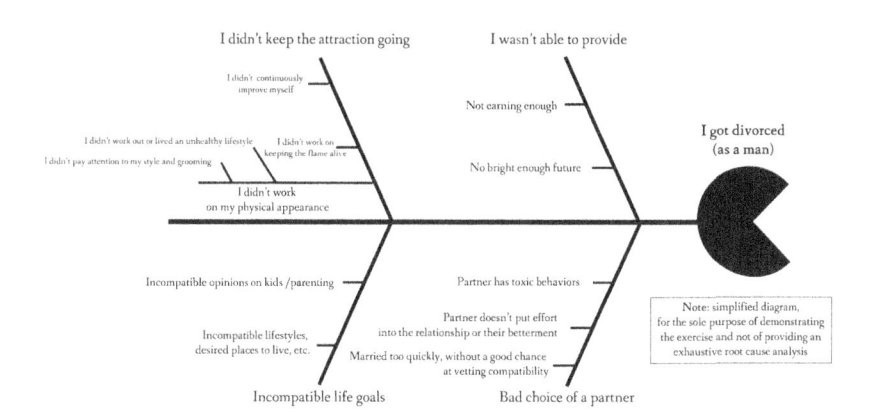

Larger images are available at Luca-Dellanna.com/fishbone

NOTES ON THE EXAMPLE DIAGRAMS

Due to the constraints of creating a small yet clear picture, the previous diagrams are not a comprehensive list of all possible root causes but only show the top ten or fifteen. Most probably, while reading them, you noticed at least a few important omissions.

That's okay. The important is you got the gist of the exercise and are ready to reproduce it for your own goals.

Fishbone diagrams are useful. They take more time than simple pre-mortems but are more complete. The practice of dividing the fish spine into four or six "main bones" representing categories of root causes and then dividing the main bones into many smaller ones forces you to be more exhaustive in your analysis, which in turn reduces your blind spots.

It is crucial you perform this exercise in written form. The act of drawing the bones and splitting them into smaller ones helps you consider all possibilities. Moreover, it yields a drawing to show your partner, friend, or colleague to get their comments and further reduce your blind spots.

Try the fishbone diagram exercise on your most important long-term goal. I promise it will lead to at least one major insight that will dramatically increase your chances of achieving it.

Remember: the fishbone head contains not a desired success but a hypothetical failure – for the same reason why studying failures is just as important as studying successes, if not more.

40

MANAGING BETS

For most successful people, a defining project propelled them to stardom: Mark Zuckerberg's *Facebook*, J.K. Rowling's *Harry Potter,* Travis Kalanick's *Uber*, etc. But most often, it wasn't clear at the beginning that it would become the defining project of their life. It started as "just another project."

Uber was just one of many projects Kalanick juggled in 2010.

Zuckerberg started quite a few software projects before Facebook. Sure, most of those were tiny, but was it so obvious before the fact that Facebook would have become so big? Probably, for at least some time, it looked like "just another project."

And J.K. Rowling wrote another novel and more minor projects before her world-famous Harry Potter.

Most successful people start with a *portfolio* of bets that later converge to a single, major, winning bet. The keyword is "later."

You don't necessarily need to work on many bets at once, but you must entertain the possibility you might have to work on many bets before one succeeds. And so, have a strategy considering that.

BETS AND STRATEGIES

In this book, I use the term "bet" very liberally to refer to any activity that might or might not work: a project, a job, a romantic date, or even spending some time in a new city.

Strategies are made of a series of bets.

Even in strategies that succeed at the first try, that first try was a bet, even though it doesn't seem like it in hindsight.

Failure to acknowledge that ***all* strategies comprise a series of bets** causes us to go all-in on a single project that might fail.

Instead, good strategies *always* (always!) consider the possibility that our first few attempts might fail – otherwise, they're bets, not strategies.

Therefore, good strategies avoid going all-in on any single project and assume that more than one project will be required to succeed (though, obviously, the fewer tries, the better).

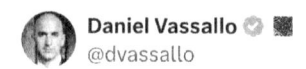

> **Daniel Vassallo** ✓
> @dvassallo
>
> Work under uncertainty:
> - Hard work → Trial & error
> - Focus → Many things at once
> - Optimization → 80/20 rule
> - Consistency → Intensity
> - Avoid distractions → Embrace randomness
> - Practice 10,000 hrs → 100 bets
> - Goals → Stay in the game
> - Efficiency → Slack in the system
>
> 5:03 AM · Mar 31, 2022

A tweet by David Vassallo, founder of the Small Bets community.

MANAGING YOUR BETS

In Part IV, we have already seen how, given a single project, it is hard to know whether you should stick with it for longer or abandon it to move to the next bet. However, you can look at patterns in your behavior across projects, such as whether you *always* drop projects early or you *never* drop projects voluntarily, and use this information to consider adjusting your approach in the opposite direction of your past patterns.

MY STRATEGY: ALTERNATING

As an author, I constantly have the following dilemma: should I work on a new book idea, or should I promote my latest one?

My solution is simple: I spend half of my time developing new ideas and half of my time expanding on the one idea that got me the most success so far.

This framework might enable you to both consider new ideas and develop a project long enough so that its fruits can blossom.

Of course, do not take the "half/half" literally. It can be 70/30, 30/70, or any other split. Not even I take the split too seriously, as I often work for weeks on a single side of it. What matters is the general principle: alternating is better than either extreme.

BETWEEN BETS

What matters in the short term is a bet's outcome. **But in the long term, all that matters is whether the current bet made your future bets more likely to succeed** – perhaps because of the know-how you learned or the trust and relationships you built.

Develop the habit of designing, executing, and evaluating your bets to maximize the learnings and long-term assets you get out of them *(knowledge, skills, habits, trust, relationships, etc.)*

Hence, here is an important question to ponder:

How many bets must you make in order to learn enough to make your success inevitable?

How many speeches must you make to become a good public speaker? How many products do you need to launch to become a competent entrepreneur?

How many failures do you need to succeed? Ensure you have a strategy that can afford that number of attempts.

Hopefully, you will succeed faster, maybe even on your first try. But if you want your success to be inevitable, you must be able to afford to make many attempts – and start making them as soon as possible.

LEARN FROM YOUR FAILURES

On the one hand, you want a strategy enabling you to make many attempts, but on the other hand, you want to succeed as fast as possible, which requires **making your failures as big a step forward as possible.**

Here are a few ideas to achieve that:

1. **Use your bets to experiment:** test your assumptions, try a new approach, and gather information about what works and what doesn't.
2. **Use your bets to build skills, relationships, trust,** and other assets that last in time. They will make your future bets more likely to succeed.
3. **Never risk your long-term assets.** No bet of yours should, in case of failure, destroy your health, capital, relationships, and trustworthiness.

Do take short-term bets, but always take them as part of your long-term strategy, so that they support it rather than impair it.

PERFECTIONISM AND ITS OPPOSITE

Perfectionism is problematic because it limits the number of attempts you will make in your lifetime. That said, the opposite of perfectionism is problematic too. Doing things too badly won't help you progress.

Find the sweet spot where you put enough effort to allow good things to happen but not so much effort that you reduce the number of good things you can make happen.

The trick to finding this sweet spot is to stop considering activities and projects one by one and instead consider them as an iterated game.

To understand what I mean, look at the following two charts (which, obviously, are qualitative and not quantitative).

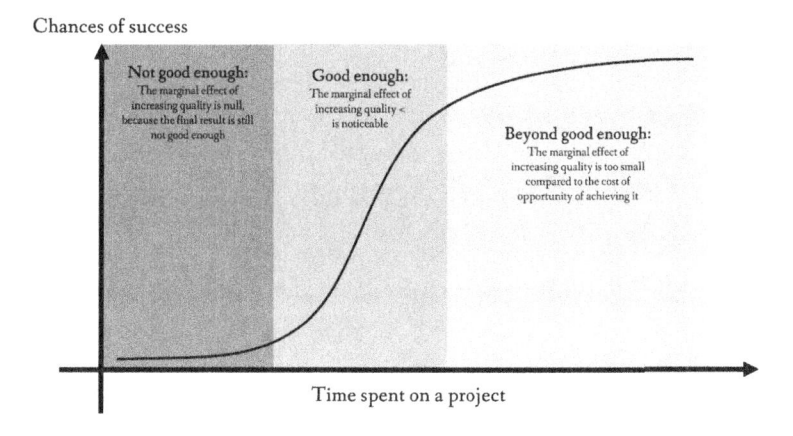

[Chart: Chances of success vs. Time spent on a project, with three regions:
- **Not good enough:** The marginal effect of increasing quality is null, because the final result is still not good enough
- **Good enough:** The marginal effect of increasing quality is noticeable
- **Beyond good enough:** The marginal effect of increasing quality is too small compared to the cost of opportunity of achieving it]

The chart above refers to a single project. By itself, it's not very actionable. But consider the second chart, which takes into account that the less time you spend on a single project, the more you can undertake.

Chances that at least one project succeeds

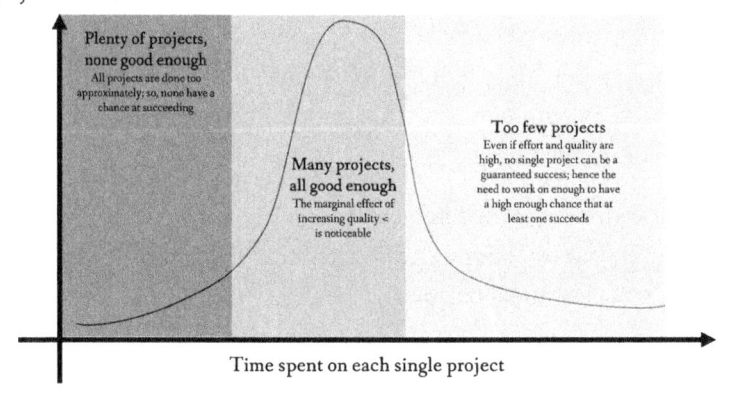

Plenty of projects, none good enough
All projects are done too approximately; so, none have a chance at succeeding

Many projects, all good enough
The marginal effect of increasing quality is noticeable

Too few projects
Even if effort and quality are high, no single project can be a guaranteed success; hence the need to work on enough to have a high enough chance that at least one succeeds

Time spent on each single project

These two charts show a counterintuitive principle. If you want to maximize a project's chances of success, work as much as possible on it. But if you want to maximize *your* chances of success, work on as many projects as possible, *but enough on each to achieve a good enough level of quality to give them a proper chance to succeed.*

Of course, no precise formula exists to know how much time and effort to pour into a project. But you want to structure your projects so that you get as fast as possible an answer to whether that will be the project that will bring you what you seek.

This often consists of reducing the scope of the project to test as early as possible whether there is compatibility between your skills and the demand for your project (e.g., whether your skills and project match what the market wants, or whether what you can bring to a relationship matches your partner's needs and the other way around).

HOW MANY BETS DO YOU NEED?

While some entrepreneurs succeed with their first product, many others need to iterate on their product a few times, or even a few dozen times. And while some entrepreneurs succeed with their first startup, others succeed with their second, third, fifth, or tenth one.

The same applies to authors, people dating, etc.

Of course, hopefully, you will succeed with your first or second bet. But more likely, you will succeed with your third or thirtieth one.

Your strategy must allow you to take many bets if needed.

This requires you to pay attention to two considerations:

1. Play each bet with the required urgency to still have time to play many others (though without rushing it to the point that you can't work on it well enough to give it a chance to succeed)

2. Be reasonably frugal with your time, money, trust, and other assets so that you keep enough to afford many other bets.

Too many people fail because they excessively consume their financial capital, social capital, health, or time left, preventing them from taking further bets.

Be more frugal and risk-conservative. Reliably winning long-term games requires being able to play many times.

CHAPTER SUMMARY

Most long-term strategies require you to take enough bets that might not work to have a good chance that at least one brings you the success you want.

For those strategies to work reproducibly *for you*, you must guarantee you can take many bets.

This requires you not to spend too much time and resources on each bet and to take those bets in such a way that their failure does not preclude your ability to take further bets.

41

MIXED FEELINGS

"Your brain knows what to do only when it has a clear association about what it needs to avoid and what it needs to move toward.

For money, we often send mixed signals [...], and **when you give your brain mixed messages, you're going to get mixed results.**"

— *TONY ROBBINS*

There are many reasons why you might procrastinate on a task once. But if you procrastinate on the same task twice or more, it's usually a sign that you are uncomfortable with it.

Unless you address the uncomfortableness, you will procrastinate the task indefinitely – or at least until it's too late.

. . .

There are two main reasons a task might feel uncomfortable, and the rest of this chapter addresses them:

1. You associate mixed values or emotions with an action or outcome.
2. You aren't convinced that completing the task is worth the effort.

MIXED VALUES

Here are a few examples of how mixed values associated with an action or outcome can withhold action:

– You want to get rich but also think wealthy people are generally evil or unhappy.

– You want to sell your product or service but also believe that selling means pestering people.

– You want to dress attractively but also associate that with morally-lose people.

– You want to have sex but also associate it with sin or STDs.

– You want to ask a question, but whenever you did it in the past, your former boss would get angry or make a fool out of you.

In all the cases above, mixed values or mixed emotions prevent you from taking action or doing it with the conviction required to succeed.

Ask yourself if you have mixed feelings or emotions associated with the actions you must take to succeed.

If so, do not ignore this limitation. It might be an emotional limitation, but it's a limitation nevertheless, and it will keep limiting you until you address it.

CORRECTING MIXED VALUES OR EMOTIONS

I do not know of a single solution that always works, but here are two options that do work relatively often:

1. **Spend time with virtuous people who already do what you need to do.** For example, if you have mixed values associated with selling, spend some time with salespeople who genuinely help people. Or, if you have mixed feelings associated with acquiring wealth, spend some time with wealthy people who are also good people. Even just a one-hour conversation might be enough to convince you that it is possible to achieve success without compromising your values.

2. **Find a way to do what you must do in the easiest and most pleasurable way possible.** If you do not like building professional relationships, do not try to attend large conferences yet: that might be too much. Instead, look for a smaller and easier step, such as inviting your favorite senior colleague for coffee. If that goes well, you will start building positive emotional associations, which will chip away at the negative ones you might have had.

Whenever you feel paralyzed, take a step back and look for a smaller step forward, prioritizing momentum before effectiveness. (Of course, *after* you achieve momentum, you want to focus on effectiveness, but until then, prioritize getting started and building positive emotional associations with what you are uncomfortable with.)

WHAT IF IT'S NOT WORTH IT?

Another common reason for procrastination is that you are not convinced that a given action is worth the time and effort.

Or, more subtly, you might believe it is worth the time and effort *in general, but not for you.*

For example, someone who cannot get themselves to exercise regularly might believe that if they did, they would get fitter. And they might believe that, for most people, it would be worth it. But they might not be convinced that *for them,* a life where they exercise and get fit would be better than a life where they don't exercise and don't get fit. Maybe they really like the free time they get from not exercising, or they really dislike going to the gym!

It is not a logical evaluation but an emotional one. Therefore, logical arguments do not influence it.

Using logic to convince yourself will only convince the non-emotional part of your brain (which is probably already convinced). Instead, use experiences to convince the emotional part of your brain.

Do what the previous page suggested: spend time with people who regularly benefit from what you aren't convinced of doing and/or figure out a smaller step forward, prioritizing actionability over effectiveness.

42

COMMITTING TO THE LONG TERM

The previous chapter, "Mixed Feelings," introduced the importance of being committed.

However, just as a previous chapter introduced the difference between High-Quality Success and Low-Quality Success, there is also such a thing as High-Quality Commitment and Low-Quality Commitment.

Low-Quality Commitment occurs when someone declares a long-term time horizon but keeps their actions mostly in the short term. For example, managers who say they have a long-term time horizon but spend most of their time putting off fires and none training their subordinates, or investors who say they have a long-term time horizon but spend most of their time finding short-term bets.

Conversely, High-Quality Commitment occurs when someone declares a long-term time horizon *and their actions match this preference.* For example, managers who spend most of their time training their subordinates and building long-term capabilities, or investors who spend most of their time finding opportunities with the potential for long-term growth and building long-term relationships.

In short, you cannot judge your commitment by your words, goals, or even your strategy. You can only judge it by the choices you make and the actions you take.

What do your actions say about your commitment? Is it low- or high-quality?

> It's a bad sign whenever you start worrying about 'the next quarter' because it proves you don't have enough conviction to not even care about 'the next quarter.'"
>
> — *IAN CASSELL*

The quote not only provides an example of evaluating your commitment by your actions but also shows that **unless you took long-term actions during the previous months, it will be hard, if not impossible, to focus on the long term this month.**

It's a vicious circle. And like all vicious circles, the key to stopping it is to take the action that breaks it *even when there's no time or energy to take it.* For example, train your people even if you feel like you don't have the time. That will lead to fewer fires to put off in the future and, therefore, more time for you to take longer-term actions.

43

COMMITTING TO THE LONG TERM WHILE RETAINING FLEXIBILITY

If you dislike long-term commitments, I have some good news: playing the long term does not necessarily mean making long-term commitments. For example, being nice to customers, getting to know them, creating goodwill, and building trust are all actions that only make sense if you are committed to the long term but are not long-term commitments that reduce your flexibility.

Of course, do not take actions that are disproportionately costly in absolute terms. For example, do not buy the highest-tier professional gear for your first month of practicing a new sport. Doing so would not only be very inefficient but also constitute a major loss if you were to change your mind and decide to move to another sport.

Instead, do engage in *habits* that only make sense with a longer time horizon: ask questions, learn skills, build trust and relationships, etc.

Committing to the long term means rejecting the shortcuts that would make sense if you were there for the short term and starting the habits that would make sense only if you were there for the long term.

44

LEARNING & ADAPTATION

Playing the long game requires a lot of learning and adapting. You do not know yet everything you need to know to succeed, but if you collect the missing knowledge along the way, you will become the kind of person who gets the kind of success you seek.

Moreover, your current plan is probably not complete nor correct enough to bring you where you want to be, but if you adapt it along the way, keeping yourself on a trajectory toward success, you will almost inevitably get there.

This chapter contains practical tips to help you learn and adapt. But remember two general principles:

1. **Learning and adaptation should be built into your strategy.** Any strategy that does not include enough time and margin of error to learn and adapt along the way is not a serious strategy.

2. **Play iterated games so they produce learning and adaptation.** Structure your tasks and interactions so that you learn from them and make future ones more effective.

METAPRACTICE

Why do some people develop a skill very fast initially but then stop making meaningful progress?

Sometimes, the reason is that they stopped practicing the skill. They only use it to get things done, but they no longer care about improving.[i]

Another reason is that when they do practice, they just focus on improving the skill.

Conversely, when long-term players practice, they focus on improving both their skill *and their practice.*

They ask themselves, "Am I learning enough from practice? If not, how can I tweak my practice to learn more out of it? Should I take notes? Should I record my practice? Should I get a mentor or trainer? Should I set objectives at the beginning of the practice?"

Do not just practice your skills. Also practice your practice.

I call this *Metapractice*.

SURRENDER

> "We do not choose our gifts. They choose us. A mark of maturity is surrendering to the person you actually are instead of the one you wish you were. Most people never get such clarity, and they're stunted for life. [...] Surrender to your gifts."
>
> — DAVID PERELL

First of all, let me clarify that "surrendering to who you are" does not mean you won't have to learn and grow. Obviously, to achieve your goals, you will have to improve yourself – believing otherwise is delusional.

Instead, "surrendering to who you are" means accepting the ways in which who you are can help you achieve your goals – even if those ways aren't exactly how you imagined you'd get happiness and fulfillment.

Here are two underrated ways in which people fail:

1. **Refusing to surrender to their gifts.** Some people do not merely want to succeed; they want to succeed *in a very specific way.* So, they unnecessarily restrict their options or stack their odds against them. *I often say that you cannot choose the cards you're dealt, but you can choose which game to play with them.*
2. **Refusing to learn the lessons the world tries to teach them.** Chronic frustration is a common symptom of stubbornness.

THE EFFORT TRAP

A common bottleneck to learning is what I call **the *effort trap:* the belief that through sheer effort, we can overcome that thing we know we need to learn but don't want to.**

This belief is problematic for three reasons:

1. Often, effort is not enough. Either you learn the lesson you don't want to learn or will keep failing. *(Paraphrasing Paulo Coelho: failure is the world's way of teaching you a lesson you don't want to learn.)*
2. At the beginning of your career, you can overcome problems caused by the lessons you don't want to learn through a bit of effort. But as you proceed through life, overcoming problems through effort alone takes more and more effort – and you will have less and less time to do so.
3. Even if effort alone could be enough as an alternative to learn a lesson we don't want to learn, the required effort is so large that it comes with massive opportunity costs. You will proceed so slowly that you won't be able to undertake enough bets or projects to make your success inevitable.

Notice when you use effort to overcompensate a lesson you don't want to learn.

Then, surrender to that lesson.

Or to the consequences of not learning it.

---

i. This is often the symptom of a shortened time horizon and/or lost faith in the idea that improving one's skill will meaningfully improve their quality of life. For example, some people do not exercise because they do not believe they can get fitter. But many more do not exercise because they do not believe that getting fitter would improve their life enough to offset the time and effort required to workout. **The bottleneck isn't whether practicing will improve their skills but whether the improvement from practice will improve their quality of life.**

45
DON'T BE TOO SMART

"90% of success can be boiled down to consistently doing the obvious thing for an uncommonly long period of time without convincing yourself that you're smarter than you are."

— *SHANE PARRISH*

Many people succeed thanks to some kind of innovation that gave them an edge.

But plenty more talented people have failed to achieve success because they have spent too much time trying to reinvent the wheel.

I'm not saying you shouldn't innovate – if you can, great!

However, innovation has opportunity costs and introduces risks.

Therefore, **only innovate as little as possible and leverage the already existing as much as possible.**

DO NOT REINVENT THE WHEEL

I'm confident in your ability to reinvent the wheel. Still, the question is not whether you are capable, but whether it's worth it.

And in particular, the question is not whether the new wheel is better than the old one, but whether it is so much better that it was worth the time and effort to develop it.

Many innovations pass the first test but not the second one.

RISK

Reinventing the wheel comes with another undesirable property: whatever you invent will be less reliable than the tried-and-tested solution.

Obviously – it's called "tried and tested" for a reason.

Again, this doesn't mean that you should not innovate. Instead, it means you probably lack the time to deal with the effort, testing, and maintenance required by more than one or two innovations.

So, be extremely deliberate and conservative with how much you innovate, and do not reinvent more than one or two wheels.

THE PLEASURE OF INNOVATION

Many of us, including myself, love innovation and think of ourselves as artisans or craftspeople directly involved in all steps of our product.

If our definition of success involves being a craftsperson, this is great! However, if it involves major financial success or impact at scale, we might have to evolve from artisans to entrepreneurs and/or scale our products or services, which almost necessarily means using as many standard components as possible except the one or two innovations that are the biggest differentiators.

A HOBBY

For some of us, innovation is what we are the most passionate and proud about in our business.

However, we should treat unnecessary innovations as a hobby. If we want to do it outside our "work hours," great. But we should never work on over-innovation *instead* of working on the core project. Nor should we let over-innovation delay our journey toward success.

46

COMMON GOALS AND HOW TO MAKE THEM MORE REPRODUCIBLE

In this chapter, I examine a few common goals and write a few thoughts on how I approach them (or would approach them) to make them more reproducible.

The discussion of each goal is not meant to be exhaustive – otherwise, each goal would require a standalone book! Instead, the objective of this exercise is just to provide you, the reader, with some examples of how the concepts illustrated in this book could be applied to real-life goals.

If there's any specific goal you would like me to write about, let me know by emailing me at Luca@Luca-Dellanna.com

GOAL #1: A BRILLIANT CAREER

First of all, I would be more specific about what this goal entails. Is it the earnings potential, the professional fulfillment, or the prestige?

Then, I would ask myself **what careers are Pareto-Frontier-optimal for what I seek.** For example, if I didn't care about prestige but cared a lot about earnings, I would ask myself, what careers are not prestigious but pay well?

I would also consider any values or constraints of mine. For example, if I cared about spending quality time with my family, I would ask myself, what careers pay well but allow me to be home early every evening? This might seem banal, but many people miss this step and regret it later.

Once I defined my preferred career, I would apply some of the learnings from the "Derisk, derisk, derisk" chapters. I would ask myself, what are common reasons why people in this career fail or drop out, and what can I do to prevent them?

I would also make a *pre-mortem:* let's imagine I follow my preferred career but fail to progress. What could have happened, and what can I do about it now? Drawing a *fishbone diagram* might also help.

Finally, I would consider goals and risks *outside* of my career. For example, in which ways might I end up unhappy even if I achieve my professional goals?

GOAL #2: GETTING A PROMOTION

I know – this is a sub-goal of the previous page's objective. But this is the beauty of the *derisk, derisk, derisk* approach: just like a fractal, you can apply it at multiple levels to improve your chances of success at each.

First of all, it's important to prevent your career from becoming a race to the bottom. Hence, begin by determining your boundaries and, only afterward, draft a plan to get a promotion while remaining within those boundaries.

Another critical consideration is that there are many ways to get a promotion, but only some *also* increase your chances of getting the following promotion. These are the approaches that avoid taking shortcuts and instead rely on building skills, trust, and a solid reputation.

Then, as usual, I would *derisk, derisk, derisk* by asking myself, what are the possible reasons that talented and determined people fail to achieve a promotion? Common answers include focusing on demonstrating one's competence at their current job while forgetting to also demonstrate competence at their next one, failing to build the right relationships and a reputation of reliability and proactiveness, or working for a boss or company that aren't growing or supportive of their employees' growth.

Finally, I would regularly ask myself, "What does my trajectory look like? And is it leading me where I want to be, fast enough and with enough certainty? If not, what changes should I make?"

GOAL #3: LAUNCHING A SUCCESSFUL PRODUCT

No matter how talented and hard-working you are, you cannot guarantee that your first product will be successful. It might take a few, or even several – both for you to find something others want, for you to develop the skills to build it, and for you to grow your audience and reputation so that you can distribute it to those who would buy it.

Hence, your primary focus should be on launching as many products as required to produce a success. This requires, among others, keeping your expenses low (so that you can afford to stay in this career for longer and thus launch more products) and iterating on them fast enough.

That said, there are entrepreneurs who do launch product after product yet fail to succeed. To prevent this, your secondary focus should be on ensuring that each product you launch builds long-term assets – for example, your skills, reputation, audience, or relationships.

No plan is perfect, so you should also constantly review your execution. Are you progressing fast enough? Are you growing your skills, audience, and reputation?

Finally, as usual, *derisk, derisk, derisk.* Study how others with a similar objective to yours failed. Learn from their mistakes before they become your mistakes.

GOAL #4: A HAPPY RETIREMENT

Being this a very broad objective, I would begin with being more precise in its definition. What does a happy retirement mean to you?

For example, let's say it means being healthy, having a loving family, and being financially comfortable. We should plan for each of these three sub-objectives separately yet continuously check that our plan to achieve one won't cause detriment to the others.

Let's work on the sub-objective of being healthy, and let's reverse-engineer it. What does it mean, for you, to be healthy at 80 years? And what does that translate to in the present? For example, let's say that, for you, being healthy at 80 means being able to climb a flight of stairs in one go. Given the well-known phenomenon of sarcopenia – the loss of muscle mass and strength that occurs as we age – how many flights of stairs should you be able to climb in one go *now,* at your current age? According to Dr. Peter Attia's book *Outlive,* which inspired this example, to be able to comfortably climb stairs when you are 75, you need to be in the top 5% of people by cardiovascular fitness. Are you there yet? And if not, what should you start doing to get there as soon as possible?

Remember: the power of derisking and, in general, the contents of this book is all about detecting problems before they are painful and while you still have time to address them. I always say that *problems grow the size they need for you to acknowledge them. If* you want an easy life with only small problems, strive to acknowledge them as early as possible.

GOAL #5: INVESTING

If investing were my core occupation, here are a few considerations I would make.

First of all, I would clarify my time horizon – is it 1 year, 10 years, or 30 years? Not only should this be a fundamental factor in deciding my investing strategy, but I should also avoid comparing myself against anyone with a shorter time horizon – if I did so, I might be misled into taking a quantity of risk that's optimal for them but suboptimal for me.

Secondly, I would figure out what long-term assets I must build to succeed. Financial capital, obviously, but what else? Skills? Access to investing opportunities? Relationships?

Thirdly, I would *derisk, derisk, derisk* by asking myself how other investors failed. I would be careful to consider both bad investing decisions and bad non-investing decisions – the latter including both work-related non-investing decisions, such as hiring a bad advisor, and non-work-related decisions, such as neglecting their health.

Finally, I would set myself periodic reminders to evaluate my trajectory – not just based on my recent outcomes but also on a broader evaluation of the long-term assets I built, the risks I took, and the sacrifices I made. Based on this broader evaluation, what does my trajectory look like, and is it leading me where I want to be, with a good enough distribution of outcomes? If not, what changes should I make?

ACKNOWLEDGMENTS

To my family, for the love and support they gave me. In particular, to my wife, **Wenlin Tan,** for the love and joy she brings to my life, and for how she makes it easier and more enjoyable. To my mother, **Martine,** for supporting and loving me all my life, and to **Franco,** for loving her. To my father, **Riccardo,** for the same and for stirring intellectual curiosity within me. I wish he hadn't passed away so early; we would have had tons to talk about. To my parents-in-law, **Tan Mui Siong and Tan Siew Hong,** for raising the love of my life and accepting me as part of their family. And to my dog **Didi,** for his loyal friendship and the happiness and joy he brings to my life.

To **Guy Spier,** for the conversations, encouragement, and support, and for bringing my attention to parts of my life and work that I neglected, and for embodying many of the principles of playing the long-term – his example is inspiring. My thanks also go to his team (in particular, **Chantal Hackett, David Jud,** and **Mariana Baldé**) and to the ValueX community he put together, for the support and exchange they provided.

To **Jim O'Shaughnessy,** for the chats in which we discussed reproducibility and his enthusiastic support.

To **David Vassallo** & the Small Bets community, for the support, idea exchange, and for stewarding some of the principles discussed here.

To **Bogumil Baranowski,** for inviting me to his podcast to talk about this book.

To **Nassim Nicholas Taleb,** for giving me the rigor to notice survivorship bias and, in general, to think more clearly.

To **Ole Peters,** for his work on ergodicity that helped me see the difference between the average outcome and *my* outcome.

To **Lance Johnson, Wenlin Tan,** and everyone else who heard or read early versions of these concepts, and helped me clarify my thinking or encouraged me to write more about it.

To my friends and everyone else who, directly or indirectly, knowingly or unknowingly, contributed to my well-being.

To my Patrons, **Scott Mitchell** and **Pablo Cárdenas.** Their help gave me stability on which I could conduct my research.

Unless noted otherwise, all images come from Pixabay, Unsplash, or Wikimedia Commons, or have been generated with Midjourney or PlaygroundAI.

Luca, his wife Wenlin, and their dog Didi.